017-So

19F

Software Development:
Fashioning the Baroque

# Software Development: Fashioning the Baroque

Darrel Ince

*Computing Discipline, Faculty of Mathematics*
*The Open University*
*Milton Keynes, UK*

OXFORD    NEW YORK    TOKYO
OXFORD UNIVERSITY PRESS
1988

Oxford University Press, Walton Street, Oxford OX2 6DP
Oxford New York Toronto
Delhi Bombay Calcutta Madras Karachi
Petaling Jaya Singapore Hong Kong Tokyo
Nairobi Dar es Salaam Cape Town
Melbourne Auckland
and associated companies in
Berlin Ibadan

Oxford is a trade mark of Oxford University Press

Published in the United States
by Oxford University Press, New York

British Library Cataloguing in Publication Data
Ince, D. Darrel
Software development: fashioning the
baroque.—(Oxford science publications).
1. Computer systems. Software. Development
I. Title
005.1
ISBN 0–19–853757–3
ISBN 0–19–853758–1 (Pbk.)

Library of Congress Cataloging in Publication Data
Ince, D. (Darrel)
Software development: fashioning the baroque/Darrel Ince.
1. Computer software—Development. I. Title. II. Series.
QA76.76.D47152 1988    005.1—dc19    88–18608
ISBN 0–19–853757–3
ISBN 0–19–853758–1 (Pbk.)

Printed in Great Britain
at the University Printing House, Oxford
by David Stanford
Printer to the University

# Preface

About fifteen years ago I used to go to large numbers of parties. The normal way to get to know fellow guests was to ask about jobs. When I was asked what my work was I usually told the inquirer that I was an academic. Almost invariably, the reply my fellow guest gave to this was a variation on the theme: 'Well I don't like work either!' However, when I explained that I was a computer scientist I felt that somehow my stock was raised considerably. Some of my listeners even went as far as exclaiming that I must be extremely clever. This was really an irrational reaction based on the fact that in the early 1970s computers were still regarded as a mystery.

This state of affairs has changed considerably. Computers now pervade almost all our lives; not only at work, but also in education and leisure. If I go to a party now and announce that I am a computer scientist I no longer receive reverence, what usually happens is that I have to listen to a detailed description of what my fellow guest has done with his home computer, how much RAM it has, and how he has used a certain programming trick to obtain a speed-up of his programs.

About a year ago, in order to boost my flagging ego I started to describe the real nature of my job: that I was a software engineer. Again I received no reverence. The most common reply was: 'What's that?'. This book, which contains a series of essays, is an attempt to explain.

Producing a large software system is the most challenging technical activity that the human race attempts to carry out. Software systems are massively complex and the production process is fraught with problems that do not occur in other engineering disciplines. In writing this book I have had three aims. First, I have attempted to explain why software development is so difficult. Second, I have tried to describe some of the work that is being carried out by both developers and researchers in an attempt to reduce the problems that occur. Third — and this is a minor theme — I have tried to explain that you cannot divorce software development from social, economic, and political factors, and that not taking into account such factors can lead to disasters as big as those that occur when technical issues are ignored.

I have deliberately written the book in such a way that both the lay-person and the informed reader can understand it. Unfortunately, this will mean that, very occasionally, the more informed reader may feel a little impatience at detailed explanations of familiar concepts. However, I hope that, because the major bulk of this book contains new material that is only reported in academic journals or internal company reports, that the more technically literate readers will regard this as a minor inconvenience.

A number of people deserve my thanks for enabling me to write this book: my wife, Stephanie, who has put up with my frequent absences; John Rumens who helped with the title; and Professor Richard Housden who provided the conditions necessary for me to put this book together.

I would also like to thank the editor of *The Independent* for permission to reproduce the article which forms the basis of Chapter 2 and the editor of *Accountancy* for permission to reproduce the article which forms the basis of Chapter 15. My thanks are also due to the EEC Esprit programme for providing the funds for me to work on project MUSE; and which enabled me to write Chapter 3.

Milton Keynes
1988

D.I.

# Contents

# 1

# The problem with software

Before I get into the heart of the book and describe some of the developments in software technology that have occurred in the 1980s, a tutorial would seem to be in order. Many of you will only have a hazy knowledge of how industrial software development is carried out. The first part of this chapter will describe the best of current practice, give you a vocabulary of sorts, and enable you to understand what comes after. If you work in the information technology sector then you should skip these pages.

The first document that the software developer has to process is fairly nondescript. It is known as the *customer statement of requirements*. This is an expression, from a potential customer, of what he requires of a new software system. Often this is quite a short document: it can range from one to twenty pages. In it the customer explains what the system he requires should do. This explanation is almost invariably couched in terms that are used in the application rather than in computer jargon. Thus, the statement of requirements for a financial system would normally use words such as 'account', 'share portfolio', 'discounted cost' and 'bank teller', rather than technical words such as 'module', and 'asynchronous interface'.

The statement of requirements will also describe any constraints upon the developer. A common constraint is the response time of the software: how long it takes to perform certain actions. This is particularly important in defence applications. For example, in ship-borne anti-missile defence systems where computers have to track, identify, and try to destroy an aggressor missile well before the missile hits the ship. In such an application the computer system has to respond in one or two seconds. Other typical constraints include insisting on a particular programming language to be used, or insisting on a particular computer in which the software system is to be placed.

The next stage in the software development process is called *requirements analysis* or *systems analysis*. During this activity the developer attempts to expand and amplify the statement of requirements and produce the system specification: the document that is an exact description of what a proposed system is to do. In this document, relatively abstract descriptions of a system's functions are fleshed out, expanded, and made precise. For example, the sentence 'The system should provide facilities which enable booking clerks to discover information about seat bookings for flights' might be expanded into a section of the system specification that would include the functions shown overleaf:

**1.1**    The function of the FREE_FLIGHT command is to display the next flight to a particular destination that contains empty seats. The booking clerk should type in two items of information: the destination of the flight and the class of ticket (economy, business, or first). The system will display the flight number.

**1.2**    The function of the BOOKED_PERSON command is to discover which flight a particular customer is booked on. The booking clerk should ideally type in two items of information: the customer's name (initials followed by surname) and the destination. If the destination is not known, then the second item should not be typed. The system will either display the flight number, the date of flight, and the time of the flight, or display the message ' the customer is not booked on any future flight'.

**1.3**    The function of the NOTIFY_CANCEL command is to print out on a remote printer the names and the contact addresses of the passengers for a particular flight. This command is used when a flight is cancelled or postponed and enables staff to get in contact with the affected customers. The booking clerk should type in the flight number and the date of flight. The list of affected customers will be in alphabetic order and, for each customer, should include an address and a telephone number.

In general the customer statement of requirements is expanded considerably in deriving the system specification. A factor of 10-to-1 to 20-to-1 is common. Hence, on large software projects the system specification often consists of volumes of text thousands of pages long.

Once the system specification has been constructed the developer then starts designing a system. The design is expressed in terms of modules. These are self-contained chunks of code that are the building blocks of a software system. Each usually carries out one function; for example, in a air-traffic control application, there will be modules that sense a plane's position, update the visual display unit on which plane positions are displayed and which warn when two planes come within collision distance. These modules communicate with each other by passing data to and fro.

Figure 1.1 shows the design of part of a radar system. It uses a popular graphic notation known as a structure chart.[1] Each rectangle represents a module. A line joining two modules represents the fact that these modules cooperate with each other in carrying out a task. This cooperation usually involves them passing data. For example, the module *Track_in* cooperates with the module Sensor by means of the latter passing the data item *Track_id*. The round-cornered rectangle represents a database: a store of data that can be used by any number of modules. The description of a software system in terms of its modules, their relationship with each other, and their relationship with databases is known as a *system design*.

After the system design is complete the processing that occurs in each module is specified. This activity is known as *detailed design*. It involves the designer specifying, in a step-by-step way, the detailed processing required in each module, in terms of primitive actions such as moving data into an area of the computer's memory or comparing two numeric values in parts of the computer's memory.

When detailed design is complete the developer then converts the detailed designs formed into program code. This is a relatively simple process: it involves the almost automatic conversion into statements in a programming language. The conversion is carried out by a programmer.

When coded modules are produced they are checked by executing them with test data. This is a process known as *unit testing*. After each module has been unit tested the system to be produced is gradually built up module by module. Each time a module is added to a partially built system, it is executed with test data to check that it interfaces with the other modules it cooperates with. The process of building a system gradually is known as *integration*, and the testing of a partially built system is known as *integration testing*.

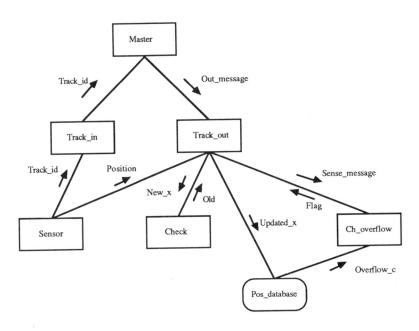

**Figure 1.1.** A software design for a radar application.

After all the modules have been added and a software system is complete the developer has to check that it meets the customer's requirements. This checking is carried out as a two-stage process. First, the whole system is executed with test data that checks out its functions.[2] This is carried out in the developer's environment with external interfaces to the system, such as chemical reactors or radar sensors, that cannot be provided directly by the developer being simulated by special-purpose hardware or by specially written software. This process is known as *system testing*. It is a preliminary check that the developer has produced the right system. For a system of any size the system test will consist of thousands of individual tests.

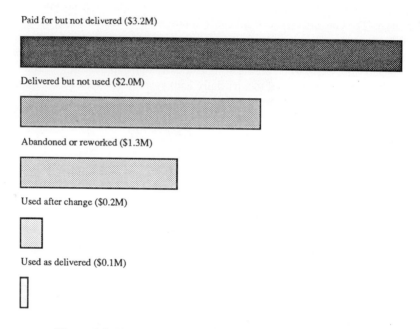

**Figure 1.2.** Figures from a study of nine systems developed for the US Government.

Second, the software system is tested in the environment in which it will be placed. Again, like system testing, this consists of thousands of tests. However, unlike system testing, it is usually carried out by the developer with the customer in attendance. When the software passes all its tests it is formally accepted by the customer. Hence, this process is known as *acceptance testing*. It is extremely serious if a software system fails one of its acceptance tests. It means that the developer has to modify the system and, since the modification may invalidate previous, successful tests the customer has every right to ask the developer to repeat all the acceptance tests from the first test. This is the reason for carrying out system testing as a preliminary to acceptance testing.

This, then, is the process known as software development, the practitioners of which are known as software engineers. The vast majority of information technology companies follow this phase-oriented means of producing systems, although the names for each phase may be different from developer to developer. It does not radically differ from the model of development used by the manufacturers of refrigerators, bridges, houses, or aeroplanes. However, there are problems with software development that are never encountered by other industries. A graphic indication of these problems is shown in Figure 1.2.

It is taken from a report produced from a US Government Accounting Office, written in 1979, that examined the fate of nine federal software projects. Of these projects only $0.1m worth of software was used as delivered. A staggering $3.2m worth of software was delivered but never used. Now these figures represent a small fraction of the American Government's budget for software in 1979 but, nevertheless, are still a graphic indication of some of the problems faced by software developers

Probably, the most comprehensive set of figures that demonstrate that there are major problems with software development were produced by Burton Swanson and Bennet Lientz, two young academics from the Graduate Management School in the University of California at Los Angeles. They were concerned with discovering the nature of a software activity known as maintenance. This term is a euphemism for the process of modifying a software system after it has been handed over to a customer. In a survey that covered 487 software developers Swanson and Lientz discovered that, on average, 48% of their staff's time was spent on maintenance, as against 43% being spent in developing software from anew. They also discovered that the maintenance effort for a number of developers was as high as 60%.

When they explored these figures further Swanson and Lientz discovered seven reasons for maintenance. These are shown in Figure 1.3. Approximately 21% (12.4+9.3) of the effort during maintenance arises from errors committed during the software production process. The large percentage figure attributed to enhancement, the modification of a system in order to improve it, also contains a figure of 25% effort required to eliminate errors due to the developer's misunderstanding what the customer required from a system. This means that at least 32% (12.4 + 9.3 + 41.8/4) of the effort involved in maintenance is solely due to rectifying errors that occur during the production process.

Both the US Government Accounting Office report and the Swanson and Lientz survey indicate that very serious problems occur during the production of software. Very rarely do products such as radios, aeroplanes, and bridges suffer from such a high level of resource expenditure in rectifying errors after they have been released to a customer. So what are the reasons for this state of affairs?

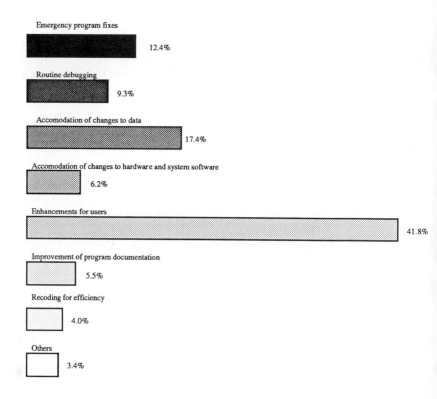

**Figure 1.3.** Burton and Leintz's figures for maintenance effort.

To explain one reason an anecdote is in order. Recently, I needed to make some changes to a software system that I had developed about four years ago. The original idea behind the software was good. However, in the intervening time other academics had carried out research that I knew would improve the software and would make it a much more flexible product.

I was extremely proud of the system. There were three reasons for my pride. First, the idea behind the software was still quite novel; it was a real contribution to software research. Second, it had proved so useful that I had received over thirty requests for copies of it from fellow academics, and even from industrial software developers. This may not seem remarkable. However, it is exceptionally rare for software developed in a university to be of any interest to outside computer scientists. Third, during the development of the system I had paid an obsessive attention to documenting it properly: I had written down exactly what the software system did; I had specified the design; I had even been very careful to write narrative text inside the program, describing what each of its sections did. I had done everything, in fact, which modern software textbooks tell us to do when developing software.

Unfortunately, when I came to change the system in order to improve it, the feeling of pride that I experienced in reading neatly-written, descriptive documents disappeared very quickly. Each change that I had planned to implement had unfortunate consequences: one change made the screen of the microcomputer's visual display unit go blank; another change put my program into a repetitive operation whereby seemingly random characters were displayed on the screen; another change gave wrong results — not just marginally wrong results, but results that could not be further away from the correct results.

My first reaction to this was to blame the passage of time. After all, I had developed almost perfect documentation for the program, and the only reason I could think of for my lack of success in modifying the system was my current unfamiliarity with it. Unfortunately, this did not prove to be so. I spent an inordinate amount of time attempting to understand the system and then re-applied the changes. This further expenditure of my time improved the situation only marginally: the screen still went blank, random characters, albeit different ones, still appeared, and the wrong results were duly obtained.

To discover what was happening I spent more time analysing what exactly happened when one change occurred. The system that I had built was neatly partitioned into modules. Each module was connected to other modules by virtue of the fact that they passed data to each other; for example, the module that controlled the dialogue with the user passed requests generated by the user to the module that determined exactly what the user wanted.

The startling fact that I discovered was that these connections were so complex that a change to one module of my system almost invariably required a change to another module; this, in turn, required a change in a further module, and so on. For the particular change that I examined in detail, nine modules needed to be modified. Unfortunately, I had missed one of these modifications and had caused the vdu screen to go blank!

The problem I had encountered could be blamed on the complexity of my system. It had reached its natural limit and its internal structure resisted any further change. This is not solely a phenomenon confined to systems developed by academics. In the early 1980s two young American academics, Sally Henry and Dennis Kafura, carried out a study of a large software system known as UNIX.[3] This is a very popular software system that was developed at Bell Laboratories. in the United States, and that controls the resources of a computer when a number of users are accessing it. It enables the users to store large amounts of data, to run programs, and to communicate with other users.

What Kafura and Henry were interested in was the relationship between some measures of complexity that they had devised, and the number of errors which occurred in the UNIX system. The aim of their research was to give software project managers the tools which enabled them to predict errors in advance of programming a system.

What they did was to apply their complexity measures to each module in the UNIX system, and then look at the changes that had been applied to it since it had been distributed to users. These changes would normally be due to programming errors that had occurred in developing the system, and that had been notified to the developers by users. Kafura and Henry discovered that their complexity measure was a good measure of the number of errors that had occurred. Unfortunately, one of their results worried them considerably: one module had an extremely high value of complexity, and yet no changes had been made to it. However, in talking to the programmers who were in charge of distributing and maintaining the operating system, they discovered that the module in question was so complex that no programmer dared change any of it for fear of disturbing the rest of the system and introducing other errors.

This, then, is one aspect of the high complexity of a software system: the effect of one module in a software system on other modules. There is another aspect: the complexity inside the modules of a software system. Figure 1.4. illustrates this. It is known by mathematicians as a *directed graph*.

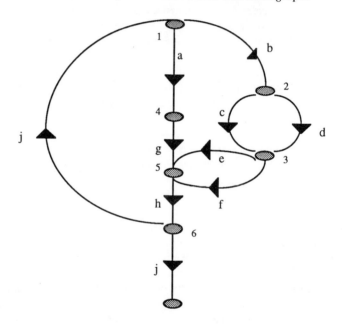

**Figure 1.4.** A graph representing the processing inside a module.

Such a graph can be used to describe what happens when a module is executed by a computer. Each small grey ellipse is known as a *node* and represents a decision inside the module. Each line is known as an *arc* and represents some processing that is to occur inside a module. For example, assume that the directed graph represents a module in a banking system whose function is to process overdrawn accounts. Node *l* represents a decision that is taken if an account is overdrawn. If the account is overdrawn then the part of the module starting with arc *a* would be executed and some processing occurs; typically, this might involve printing out a mild warning letter. If the account is overdrawn, and a letter has already been previously sent out, then decision *l* would switch processing to the part of the module starting with arc *b*. This would result in different, more drastic actions being taken. Typically, this might involve an account being closed down, and an extremely threatening letter being sent to the offending customer.

Arc *i* involves the repetition of the processing of overdrawn accounts. After an account has been examined and processed, either by the part of the module associated with arc *a* or arc *b* ,then the module returns to node 1 and another overdrawn account is examined. Arc *j* is executed when the module terminates its processing. When a module is executed, a path consisting of a number of arcs is traversed. For example, if the module processes three accounts, where only a mild warning letter is to be sent out, the path traversed would be *aghiaghiaghj*.

In order to see how complex even a simple module such as the one described above is, assume that when this module is executed that two accounts are to be processed. For two accounts there are 25 distinct paths to be executed, they are:

| | | | | |
|---|---|---|---|---|
| *aghiaghj* | *bcehiaghj* | *bcfhiaghj* | *bdehiaghj* | *bdfhiaghj* |
| *aghibcehj* | *bcehibcehj* | *bcfhibcehj* | *bdehibcehj* | *bdfhibcehj* |
| *aghibcfhj* | *bcehibcfhj* | *bcfhibcfhj* | *bdehibcfhj* | *bdfhibcfhj* |
| *aghibdehj* | *bcehibdehj* | *bcfhibdehj* | *bdehibdehj* | *bdfhbdehj* |
| *aghibdfhj* | *bcehibdfhj* | *bcfhibdfhj* | *bdehibdfhj* | *bdfhibdfhj* |

If the module processed 25 accounts then there would be 525 possible paths to be executed. If a software developer wished to test such a module and one assumes that it takes a minute to produce a set of test data, then a full exhaustive test of that module would take 180 949 134 years. In fact, things are a lot worse than this: the module discussed is extremely simple compared with those found in medium-to-large software systems, and such systems would contain hundreds, or even thousands, of such modules.

Now, in describing the complexity of a small module, my aim is not to persuade you that testing software is an inherently impossible process. Software developers have devised means of testing software relatively efficiently by executing a small subset of possible paths; the fact that there are a large numbers of highly reliable software systems in existence is direct evidence of this. My aim is to highlight the potential complexity of a software system as compared with other engineered products, such as cars and bridges.

This, then, is one aspect of the problems facing the software developer: the structural complexity of the systems that he has to produce. The major reason for this complexity arises from the functional characteristics of modern software systems. Compared with, say, the functions of a bridge, the functions that we expect of relatively small software system are orders of magnitude bigger. A bridge has one main function: to carry traffic across an obstacle, subject to values of peak and average wind speed, vehicle loading, and vehicle throughput. A small software system, say for administering the stocks of commodities in a wholesaler's warehouse, has a multitude of functions, some of them are listed below:

1. The software system should update the main database of stock levels whenever a delivery takes place.

2. Whenever a delivery takes place the system should produce delivery documentation that can be signed off by the warehouse manager.

3. The system should provide facilities whereby stores clerks are able to interrogate the main database of stock levels in order to answer customer queries.

4. The system should automatically produce order documentation whenever parts fall below a level to be determined by the warehouse manager.

5. The system should ensure that a stock level is maintained in the warehouse that is large enough to satisfy future orders but that minimizes the value of stock holdings.

6. The system should provide facilities for management at the wholesalers to interrogate the database with a view to determining purchasing strategy in the future.

7. The system should produce audit information that would allow the wholesaler's accountants to check the cash flow into and out of the company's ledger concerned with purchasing and sales.

These are a small fraction of the functions required of a commercial data-processing system. Normally, such systems would contain hundreds of functions. Commercial data-processing applications such as those found in banks, building societies, wholesalers, and insurance companies are regarded as very straightforward. Tougher application areas, such as those found defence or process control, are functionally much richer. A typical defence application, for example a missile guidance system, may contain thousands of functions.

   Major problems also arise from the nature of customer requirements and the requirements analysis process. Attempting to elicit software requirements is an extremely difficult task because of the cultural gulf between the two parties involved in the requirements analysis process. On the one hand, a customer may have detailed knowledge about his application area, but may be totally ignorant about the capabilities of information technology: on the other hand the developer may be technically superb, but have only a layman's view of the customer's proposed system.

The second reason is that the nature of requirements documents gets in the way of the transactions that have to occur between the customer and the developer, during systems analysis. A typical specification is written in English and, for large projects, usually occupies many volumes of text. English is an excellent medium for novels and poems, where the quality of such works is partly judged by the degree of ambiguity in the text. However, for a system specification, ambiguity and lack of completeness often lead to disaster. A very small example of the problems involved is shown below, it is taken from part of a system specification

1. The purpose of the system is to collect, store and analyse water level statistics from the five reservoirs managed by the water authority.

2. Sensors from each reservoir measure the water level at one-minute intervals. The values of water levels are sent to the central computer and stored.

.
.
.

13. The average level command is typed in by a research scientist. The result of typing this command is to display at the vdu the average water level for a particular reservoir. When this command is used the scientist types in the word AVLEVEL followed by the name of the reservoir and the hour required.The response to this command should be no more than 5 seconds.

The specification extract seems straightforward. Unfortunately, a close reading reveals some problems. First, what does the phrase 'and the hour required' mean? Does it mean that the user has to type in a number that represents the hour? For example, if the user types 22 does that mean 10 o'clock at night? If so how does the system know which day the time refers to? Assuming that the system stores data for a number of days, then the hour must be specified in terms of a date and an hour number.

There are other problems with the specification. First, there is an omission: it doesn't say what happens if a scientist types in the current hour. Should the system regard this as an error, or attempt to display the average of the readings up to the point when the command is typed? Clearly, this would be sensible if the scientist typed in the command during the 59th minute of an hour. However, it is meaningless when typed after the first minute of an hour. Perhaps there should be a threshold minute mentioned in the specification. After this threshold minute, the average water level up to that minute should be displayed: while before this minute a warning message should be displayed.

There is also another problem. The specification does not state what should happen when a scientist types in an hour for which no data is stored. The storage of a computer is quite limited and, consequently, only data for some hours in the past is stored. Assuming that another part of the specification details how much data should be stored, the specification should describe what happens when unavailable data is retrieved. This is a trivial example. Realistic specifications contain more subtle errors that can only be spotted by keeping details from a number of pages in the reader's head.

As well as the inherent problems of English, there is a further educational problem: many developers have been brought up within a narrow education system in which, at sixteen, students are faced with a choice of science or arts subjects. This invariably produces people who, while technically excellent, are unable to communicate effectively using the written word. Moreover, even for proficient writers, it is easy to slip into sloppy English when having to construct a large document such as a system specification.

Another problem is bound up with the size of requirements documents, a typical system specification for a medium-complexity project can run to hundreds of pages. This means that errors are almost invariably committed by both the developer and the customer because of communication problems. A large project will normally split up a specification document between a number of staff, from both the developer and the customer, with each person communicating with his opposite number, and with coordination being achieved by review and monitoring meetings. The amount of organization required to make this work is expensive and, faced with a competitive market, many developers have to skimp on this, with a consequent increase in errors.

Errors occur throughout a software project. However, errors in specifying requirements can be disastrous. When such errors are discovered during acceptance testing it usually involves the developer in very expensive re-specification, redesign, and reprogramming. These errors can be so disastrous that they have lead to software projects being cancelled before any software, imperfect or otherwise, has been delivered.

The best advice I have read about coping with fuzzy requirements was given by Fred Brookes in 1975. Brookes was a project manager on a pioneering large software project at IBM and has written a book based on his experiences. Even though it is now twelve years old at the time of writing, it is still the best book on software project management that I know of.[4] He stated that when you plan a project, you should assume that you will always throw away the first version of the software that you construct.

The initial requirements for a software system are such a problem that many commercial software developers have admitted to me in private that, at best, requirements analysis is a very tentative and fragile process. Developers who believe this invariably adopt a number of ad hoc strategies that are aimed at ensuring that, by and large, a customer gets what he wants and, at the same time, the developer makes an adequate profit. One common strategy is to add a sum that reflects the degree of risk in requirements analysis onto the estimated cost of a project. This sum would depend on the application. For example, a system for payroll administration would probably have a very small loading: such systems have been developed many times, and there is a large degree of accumulated experience in analysing the requirements for such systems. However, a system that was novel — say a defence system that used new computer hardware and controlled a novel piece of armament — would be very heavily loaded.

Other strategies are less dramatic. They include: prioritizing the functions of a system in order of importance, so that when an error in requirements is discovered in mid-project, work can be concentrated on the major functions of the developed system, with the possible result of relatively unimportant functions not being delivered; keeping project documentation on a computer so that it can be updated quickly; skimping on some activities such as unit testing in the hope that integration testing will discover any errors in coding.

Unfortunately, the software developer not only has to cope with customer requirements, which are, at best, approximate. The requirements can change during the duration of a project. It is tempting to blame this phenomena on the fickleness of the naive customer. However, the reality is that software interacts with the real world. Unfortunately, the real world is dynamic and can change quite drastically during the duration of a software project: new administrative procedures can change the requirements for an accounting system, tax changes can change the requirements for a financial reporting system, new defensive tactics by potential aggressors can invalidate many of the requirements for a missile-based anti-aircraft system. The best recent example of a project bedevilled by requirements changes was the ill-fated Nimrod project, which had to cope with over three-and-a-half thousand changes in requirements during its lifetime. Since even medium-size projects can last a few years, the project manager is continually facing the shifting sands of changes in requirements. My favourite quote about this aspect of software production process is:

(Software) development is like talking to a distant star; by the time you receive the answer, you may have forgotten the question.[5]

A number of problems in prediction occur in software projects; these are, again, due to the complexity of a software system. Probably the best known of these problems is that of estimating the cost of a project. Unlike mature engineering disciplines such as electronic engineering and civil engineering, there is no rational basis for costing a software project.

Many software developers go through a relatively organized process in arriving at an initial cost estimate. This process involves them first carrying out an initial requirements analysis and then an outline system design. Using the outline specification and design that have been produced, the developer then identifies the tasks that are required during the software project. Each task is then estimated in terms of man-hours and a labour cost is obtained by simple arithmetic. This matches the costing methods used in other industries. However, the software developer almost always invalidates this approach, by adding a 'correction' factor that can be greater than the magnitude of the cost estimate.

There are a number of reasons for this. The first is because of the uncertainties arising from fuzzy requirements and the dynamic nature of requirements. The developer does not know, at the planning stage, how accurate his initial stab at requirements is going to be, and also he will have little idea of requirements changes that will buffet his project. An experienced developer will have a good idea of the magnitude of the uncertainty, which almost invariably depends on the application area; hence he will have a sliding scale of correction factors.

The second reason for adding a correction factor is that productivity on a software project is not constant. It cannot be dictated by management. There are a host of other factors upon which productivity depends. For example, system complexity and the naivety of the user are two major factors which reduce productivity. While such factors can be identified during the planning stage, it can be very difficult to estimate exactly their effect on the cost estimate. Productivity is therefore influenced by properties of the system and the customer that are out of the control of project management.

Project output is not directly proportional to the effort and manpower put into a software project. As projects become larger and larger, the amount of communication between staff increases dramatically. Consequently, more and more time in a project will be spent in vital, but non-developmental activities, such as senior programmers communicating with designers, and designers communicating with analysts. In a small-to-medium project the increase in this overhead can be small; hence, the assumption that increasing the number of staff proportionately increases the amount of code produced will approximately hold. However, in large projects the communicational overhead rises almost to the point where gains in adding staff to a project are marginal. Fred Brookes again makes the point eloquently: [4]

> The second fallacious thought mode is expressed in the very unit of effort used in estimating and scheduling: the man-month. Cost does indeed vary as the product of the number of men and the number of months, progress does not. Hence the man-month as a unit for measuring the size of a job is a dangerous and deceptive myth. It implies that men and months are interchangeable.
>
> Men and months are interchangeable commodities only when a task can be partitioned among many workers with no communication among them.

This is true of reaping wheat or picking cotton; it is not even approximately true of systems programming.

When a task cannot be partitioned because of sequential constraints the application of more effort has no effect on the schedule. The bearing of a child takes nine months, no matter how many women are assigned. Many software tasks have this characteristic because of the sequential nature of debugging.

In tasks that can be partitioned but which require communication among the subtasks, the effort of communication must be added to the amount of work to be done. Therefore, the best that can be done is somewhat poorer than an even trade of men for months.

Many other problems in prediction occur in the software project. One typical problem occurs after system design. When this activity is complete, the project manager is faced with a document that details the modules in a system and describes the interconnection between these modules. Currently, project managers do not have any tools that enable them to determine the degree of complexity of such a design and, hence, are unable to predict with accuracy the resources needed in carrying out those activities, such as integration testing, that occur later in the software project.

Another problem in prediction occurs with errors in a software system. All but the most trivial software systems contain errors when they are released to a customer. The software developer has an obligation to ensure that these errors are eradicated. This obligation may be formal, in that it is embodied in a warranty written into the contract for the software. However, more frequently, it arises from the software developer being concerned with not losing potential customers by releasing faulty software and doing nothing to rectify this situation.

Maintenance now forms a major part of any software developer's budget; hence it would be useful to predict from the incidence of errors discovered during development what would be the incidence and nature of errors during this activity. Other engineering disciplines are well equipped with tools and methods that enable this type of prediction to take place; for example, in electronic engineering it is relatively easy to determine the probability that a circuit will break down, from defect statistics of the components that make up the circuit. Unfortunately, the research on software reliability is still in its early days.

A further disadvantage faced by software developers, as compared with, say, mechanical engineers, is the lack of tool support. The difference is so striking that it leads to massive paradoxes. For example, if you visit a modern factory you will find robots and machine tools being controlled by sophisticated computer-aided manufacturing systems for which software has been virtually crafted by hand .

Software development consists of many repetitive tasks, and automation gives the software developer the potential for large reductions in development cost. As an example of one task which would be transformed by automation, consider unit testing. Here the programmer has to test a module using real data. This testing consists of the programmer identifying paths through a module, calculating the values of test data that causes these paths to be executed, producing a file containing this data, writing a program into which the module is placed, executing the program, calculating what the correct result of the execution should, and, finally, checking the result from the execution of the module under test against this calculated value. This is an exceptionally labour-intensive process.

Unfortunately, the software project of today uses very few tools. The two tools that every project uses are a compiler and an editor. The former translates statement in a programming language into the language of the computer: the former is a tool used to modify data and programs stored in the computer. However, these are tools that have been in existence for thirty years and it is still rare to find projects that use more than these.

A further problem arises with project documentation. I have already described how English is not the ideal medium to express the function of a software system. Unfortunately, the software developer, as well as having to cope with this unpleasant fact, has to cope with problems involving other notations used on a project.

As well as needing a notation for specification, the software developer requires one for system design and one for detailed design: the expression of the processing that occurs in each module in a system. We have already seen a graphical notation for the former in Figure 1.1. An example of a notation for the latter is shown below.

```
MODULE check_balance(customer,current_balance)
Retrieve the customers current overdraft limit
IF the current balance exceeds the overdraft limit
     THEN
     Issue a warning letter to the customer
END_IF
END_MODULE
```

It describes a small module that carries out the check of the balance in a bank account. The module has a name *check_balance*, and the processing that is to occur is delimited by the words: MODULE and END_MODULE. The first line shows that the module is to process two items of data: customer and current_balance; that if the current balance exceeds the customers overdraft, then the action enclosed by the words THEN and END_IF, is to be carried out. In this case it means that a warning letter is to be sent.

There are two problems with these notations. First, there is the problem of ambiguity, lack of completeness, and inconsistency that I discussed when outlining the difficulties with specification notations. Although English plays a smaller part in notations for system design and detailed design, it still takes up a large proportion of each notation. Second, there is the problem of discontinuity. When one activity in a software project ceases, and another starts, there is a usually a notation change. For example, when requirements specification finishes and system design starts, there is usually a change from English to some graphical notation; when system design finishes and detailed design starts, there is usually a change from a graphical notation back to an English-based notation. Because of this discontinuity, major errors are often committed.

A further problem that arises from the notations used on software projects is the difficulty in demonstrating that a software system meets its specification. Obviously, this demonstration is important for the developer in terms of delivering a system that meets a contract. However, for certain categories of software it is vital. The application areas where it is virtually mandatory for a software developer to demonstrate unambiguously that software meets its specification are those with a high safety-critical element. Typically they occur in the nuclear industry, the aeronautic industry, and the chemical industry.

Software developers are at a major disadvantage compared with their counterparts in electronic engineering, civil engineering, and aeronautic engineering. For example, if a bridge falls down, a civil engineer has the mathematical tools that enable him to demonstrate that the design of the bridge satisfies the specification given to him by the customer, and that the reason for such an accident was freak winds, that were well outside the numerical limits written into the specification.

Unfortunately, many software developers are unable to provide this demonstration. The reason for this is that the mathematics that underlies software development lags well behind that of subjects such as civil engineering where, for at least a century, even school children have been calculating the forces involved in placing ladders against walls and determining the period of pendulums.

A final problem is that software is ethereal. You can't see it, or touch it, or smell it. It exists as a pattern of ones and zeros inside the store of a computer. The only time that you get an idea of what its like is towards the end of the software project, when major chunks of software have been programmed. You can at least experience it then. However, at this stage in the software project a developer will have committed something like 90% of his resources, and any mistakes discovered at this late stage can spell disaster.

These then are the problems. The software developer has to construct a product which is orders of magnitude more complex than other industrial products; moreover, he cannot experience software when late on in a project until it is too late. He is unable to pin down the requirements for a software product; indeed, the requirements can change quite drastically during the development process. Moreover, he has very limited techniques that enable him to carry out prediction, he is poorly supported by automated tools, and, at the end of the day, he cannot demonstrate unambiguously that the product that he has developed meets its specification.

Given these difficulties it seems quite a miracle that any successful software system can be built. However, much of our lives are affected by successful software systems. They, administer our bank accounts, control chemical plants, navigate aeroplanes, and control our telephone systems. The reason for this is twofold. First, human beings are wonderfully adaptable, and have a great capacity for processing complexity. Second, a large amount of resources are committed by developers in ensuring that a software system at least meets a customer's more important requirements. As much as 65% of the resources in a software project can be devoted to heavy system and acceptance testing; to reviews in which four or five staff examine documents in detail to check for errors; and to audits, where quality assurance staff ensure that a development team is carrying out the correct development processes.

Nevertheless, errors occur. Normally these are manifested as requirements that are never met. However, they can occur as serious errors detected only when a software system has been released. Three examples of typical errors are shown below.

• A fly-by-wire control system for a combat jet was not programmed to react to a certain mechanical malfunction. When the malfunction occurred the jet went out of control and crashed.

• A computer system controlling the mechanical sub-system of an aircraft issued a close door command at the wrong time. Although this did not kill anybody, this was more by luck than judgement.

• A software error occurred in a program that controlled the launch of an offensive missile from a combat aircraft. This resulted in the missile-retaining mechanism being closed before sufficient thrust had been built up for the missile to clear the wing. The pilot discovered that he had suddenly acquired an extra jet engine and his plane went out of control and crashed.

• There are a number of documented instances of programmed robots killing or maiming workers who have entered restricted areas in order to rectify errors or to carry out maintenance.

While these errors are dramatic, and are important to those affected, it must be said that they are comparatively rare. Most software companies expend an inordinate amount of resources in getting their software right. Here lies the problem. Electronics engineers can boast of productivity increases that raise computer power by an order of magnitude every few years: their counterparts in the software industry are only able to point to modest increases. A recent survey estimated the annual increase in productivity in the software industry at a negligible 4%.

The rest of this book examines many of the ideas, tools, and techniques that are being proposed in order to solve the many problems of software development. In many cases the material covered in the following chapters is still in the pre-production stage, either through being used in limited number of projects, or being examined for feasibility by industrial research laboratories, or being refined by university researchers. However, many represent promising approaches to one of the most difficult problems currently facing industry; unfortunately, one or two represent some dangerous trends.

## References

1.  For a good introduction to software engineering notations such as the structure chart see: *Software Engineering a Programming Approach*, D. Bell, I. Morrey, and J. Pugh, Englewood Cliffs, N.J.: Prentice-Hall. 1987.

2.  Although it is quite an old book, the best introduction to the process of software testing is still: *The Art of Software Testing*, G.J. Myers, New York: Wiley. 1979.

3.  Software Structure Metrics Based on Information Flow, D. Kafura and S. Henry, *IEEE Transactions on Software Engineering*, 7, 5. 1981.

4.  *The Mythical Man-month*, F.P. Brookes Jr., Reading, Mass.: Addison-Wesley. 1975.

5.  The Life-cycle — A Debate Over Alternate Models, B. I. Blum, *ACM SIGSOFT Software Engineering Notes*, 7, 4. 1982.

# 2

# The return of the hacker

One of the characteristics of software development in the 1960s was the dominant role of the hacker. A hacker was a programming magician: someone who had a detailed knowledge of a programming language and the system on which it was installed. Hackers could do unbelievable things: they could squeeze out extra hours of computer time by taking advantage of the arcane features of a computer; they could save memory size by means of programming tricks; and they could write programs that enabled novel hardware devices, such as spectrometers, to be interfaced to computers that, theoretically, had no provision for such devices. I even heard of one hacker who knew where the faulty parts of his computer were and who wrote his programs so that the data avoided these parts. I suspect that that story was apocryphal. However, it is testament to the power of the hacker that people were telling such tales. The hacker was a valuable asset to a company in the 1960s, an employee to cosset as much as a managing director or chief accountant.

However, the hacker virtually disappeared by the early 1970s. There were a number of reasons for this. First, hackers were, almost invariably, individualists; many were social misfits: college drop-outs, psychotics, and people with obsessions. They tended to work extremely well on projects where the effort could be carried out by one person. However, software projects in the 1970s had become so large that teams of staff were required, and the gains in speed and memory size made possible by hackers were more than outweighed by the corrosive effect on morale caused by their social paraplegia.

A second reason for their demise was the fact that the programs they wrote were so dense and convoluted that they were almost impossible to read. For example, hackers used computer instructions that, if documented, were contained in the updates to an appendix of an appendix to a little known section of a program manual. Consequently, when a hacker left a company, the programs that remained had properties that exactly reflected the hacker's mind: convoluted, dense, and undisciplined. These programs could not be changed to improve them or to remedy errors. If a developer was brave enough to change a hacker's program then he would have to adopt an experimental approach: try a possible change, run the system, see if it collapsed; if it did, try another change, and so on. Even if serious errors were discovered, a company would be in the embarrassing position of having to admit to all of its customers that nothing could be done.

A final reason for the end of the hackers was the nature of the errors they committed. Like other programmers, hackers committed errors; it is certainly true to say that they committed fewer errors. However, the errors they did commit were spectacular. Because hackers were continually driving deeply into the software innards of the computer, the errors they committed had global effects and were so subtle that whole teams of programming experts were required to track down the cause.

A typical hacker error occurred in the newly-developed route management system for an American railway company. The system behaved well for months. However, a particular rare combination of circumstances resulted in dozens of freight trains being mis-routed throughout America. The company had to find a large amount of resource to recover from this error. A team of software experts had the long job of tracking down an error that seemed to occur extremely infrequently, while another team travelled around the sidings of North America with the even longer job of looking for misdirected freight.

The hackers died in the 1970s when software developers started applying disciplined techniques to the production of software. A major component they used was quality assurance. Many companies set up quality assurance departments whose sole aim was to ensure that correct software was being delivered to a customer. Typically, such a department used standards, spot-checks, and reviews to ensure that a software system was correct, readable, and had been thoroughly tested. They were staffed by programmers who had met and suffered from hackers in the past and, hence, had a natural aversion to their work.

Quality assurance departments became quite powerful independent bodies, they usually had a separate reporting line to very senior management, and were capable of holding up whole projects if the staff they monitored would not mend their ways. This was not an ideal environment for the hacker. He would have some pin-striped quality assurance man breathing down his neck for most of the day, insisting that a sensible subset of a programming language be used and that he explain why he violated the programming standards of his project. If there is one thing that enrages a hacker it is the mention of standards. They are seen as a direct challenge to the creativity of the hacker, his whole *raison d'etre.*

Consequently, in the seventies a software diaspora occurred. Hackers left major companies who had invested in quality assurance and joined back street concerns or started up as one person companies. Many of the latter were extremely successful: after all, hackers were the supreme technicians. However, their use on large projects diminished considerably.

Current approaches to software development, which encompass quality assurance techniques, seem to have worked well. Considering the amount of software that is being produced in the world, there have been very few serious mishaps due to software errors. However, a set of new factors that have come into prominence over the last few years threaten the status quo.

They arise from the new-found prominence of 'user-oriented computing'. Over the last decade many users of computing systems have felt disappointed with the work of the developmental staff who are charged with providing them with a software system. Some of this disappointment was understandable. In the 1970s there was a major shortage of staff who were able to understand the software needs of users. Consequently, systems were delivered to the user that were, at best, ill-tailored, and at worst, totally inappropriate. Another reason for poor delivery was the fact that a massive culture gap existed— and still exists— between the customer and the developer. This gap resulted in the developer not understanding customer needs.

However, much of the disappointment arose from the difficult nature of software development. Software is a complex, ethereal medium that requires considerable care, and, irrespective of the talents and sympathies of development staff, slowness in delivery can never really be improved drastically. For example, there is a long period of interaction between the customer and the developer when establishing user requirements. Also, users will always have to wait for a long time for their systems because of the slow and painstaking checks required by quality assurance departments.

A major response to these problems, in the late 1970s, was to give the user much more power. This power manifested itself in two ways. The first was the introduction of a new breed of programming languages that were designed for business use and are highly interactive. They are called fourth-generation languages.[1] They contain facilities for the display of graphs, the construction of reports, and the formulation of queries on large commercial databases. I have never really been able to find out why such languages were characterized by the words *fourth-generation*. First-generation languages were just patterns of zeros and ones used in the very earliest computers: real hacker's languages. Second-generation languages replaced the zeros and ones by symbols. Third-generation languages looked very much like the mathematics we use in everyday life. In this respect fourth-generation languages don't seem to be much of a leap in difference. I suspect the term fourth-generation language is just manufacturers' hype.

The second manifestation of end-user power was the introduction of spreadsheets. These software packages have become phenomenally successful. In essence, a spreadsheet is just a square table of cells that can contain sequences of characters and numbers. Users can manipulate these cells to calculate sums, cost ratios, discounted cash flows, and other quantities indispensable to the running of a business. The spreadsheet has become incredibly successful because it matches the conceptual model the manager has of his data: for example, balance sheets, invoices, and stock records all match the basic tabular form of the spreadsheet. A recent development with larger spreadsheet packages is the inclusion of programming languages that allow the user to carry out complicated processing such as the calculation of trend statistics.

Probably the most extreme example of this trend to end-user computing is the idea of the information centre. This views the role of the computing department of a company as being solely concerned with the maintenance of a large company database. The job of the staff in such a department consists solely of ensuring that this database is stored efficiently, that the data in it is accurate, and that security violations do not occur. All the programming is done by the users using fourth-generation languages or spreadsheets.

Initially, concepts such as the information centre were hawked about by large computer manufacturers or software product companies with fourth-generation languages to sell. One can see why software product companies are keen on the idea, it is less clear why manufacturers are gung-ho about it. The answer is that fourth-generation languages soak up computer power. The information centre concept requires a large central database system that both uses massive amounts of computer time and occupies large areas of file storage. Consequently, any company that wishes wholeheartedly to embrace end-user computing has to pay out a large amount of money for hardware resources.

End-user computing is a seductive and powerful idea,[2] and is now seen by management as a panacea for the problems created by their fuddy-duddy computing departments. Each week a new fourth-generation language is announced, or a spreadsheet manufacturer announces new enhancements to an existing package, and the number of major companies embracing end-user software concepts increases dramatically. This growth has been fuelled by the relative drop in microcomputer prices, which enables non-computing departments to buy their own microcomputers and cut loose from their spoilsport computing colleagues.

This has resulted in the new age of hacking. Today's hacker differs from the hacker of the 1960s in a number of superficial ways: he dresses better and has more sumptuous accommodation; normally, he is a middle-ranking, pin-stripe executive in charge of substantial budgets, with a comfortable office and at least a substantial share of a secretary; his computing facilities are good, usually a top-range PC or a Macintosh; and he is more sociable. The hacker of the sixties was essentially a technician, dressed like a bag-man, normally lived in a cupboard, and usually had to cope with rudimentary computing equipment.

However, in essence, these two sets of hacker are the same. They are experts in the software they use, they can get the maximum performance from that software and they have the same obsessive attitude towards their programming. For example, the 1960s hacker knew how to squeeze the last few microseconds from an elderly machine; the new hacker knows how to draw little Japanese flags and Kamikaze pilots in the sales graphs generated by rudimentary graphics packages. The 1960s hacker knew how to use sections of memory that were normally cordoned off from the user; the new hacker can utilize areas of a spreadsheet normally reserved for internal purposes.

The most worrying similarity between the two categories of hacker is their propensity to make spectacular errors. At present, there does not seem to be any way of controlling the new hacker. At a recent meeting of the quality assurance departments of some of Britain's largest companies, a major worry voiced by participants was end-user quality assurance. The work of the 1960s hacker could be easily monitored and controlled by reasonably competent quality assurance staff because the hacker usually worked for a computing department. If the hacker would not submit to control then he could be sacked. However, major political problems prevent this happening to the new hacker. Computing departments and quality assurance departments are usually service organizations within a company and, consequently, have very little political clout. They are incapable of influencing the work of the more prestigious departments such as marketing, accounting, and production. For example, it is highly unlikely that a recent graduate employed in a quality assurance role would be allowed to control the computing activities of a senior accountant.

The quality assurance practitioners that I have spoken to have no answers to this problem, short of a radical reorganization of their company that would upgrade the quality assurance function. To a man, they agree that this is highly unlikely. What seems to be the answer, and it is quite a drastic answer, is to sit on the sidelines and wait for an executive to make a big mistake, *pour encourager les autres*. This recently happened in a company where a senior purchasing executive did not check the output of one of his programs and, inadvertently, ordered a massive amount of stock. The mistake, which would have seriously affected the company, was spotted by a clerk who realized that the company did not possess enough warehousing to store a tenth of the order.

So, if you are commuting into work one day and spot a large number of refrigerated wagons in a siding with a murky liquid dripping from them, or notice in your newspaper that a company is in trouble because it misvalued its assets or liabilities, then you might be looking at one of the less welcome results of end-user computing. If, in viewing such events, you are tempted to despair, don't. They benefit two categories of deserving professions: writers, like myself, desperate for colourful copy, and quality assurance departments, who are attempting to bring a little sanity into the world by pointing out that software development is too complex, too risky, and too error-prone to be anything but a thoroughly professional activity.

# References

1.  For a comprehensive discussion of these languages see: *Fourth Generation Languages, Vols I and II*, J. Martin, Englewood Cliffs, N.J.: Prentice-Hall. 1982.

2.  For an eloquent discussion of the concept of end user computing see: *Application Development Without Programmers*, J. Martin, Englewood Cliffs, N.J.: Prentice-Hall. 1982.

# 3

# Software that rusts

If you consult any management book to find out what exactly the subject is about, you will find a rare agreement on one thing: that an important component of any manager's job is prediction. Certainly, the best managers that I have met have had an almost uncanny ability to smell trouble a long way off. They can look at a statement of requirements and know that a project will threaten their family life; they can examine a design, and sense that the software represented will give them major headaches during maintenance; they can see, in a set of test reports, software that is going to give an unacceptably high level of error incidence.

Of all the areas where prediction is important, nowhere is it more important than in managing software projects, where the risks and pay-offs are dangerously high. Unfortunately, compared with managers in other industries, such as banking, accountancy, and insurance, the quantitative skills for this task have been unavailable. Compared with, say an insurance manager with his actuarial tables that provide high-accuracy estimates of life expectancy, the software project manager is nowhere. However, recent research in software engineering is promising to come to his aid.

The research is in an area of software engineering known as software metrics.[1] A metric is some measurable quantity extracted from a software project. There are two types of metric: predictor metrics and result metrics. A result metric usually measures some aspect of a software project that consumes resources; for example, the amount of time spent reading the program code for a set of modules is a result metric. A predictor metric is a measure extracted in a software project, usually from a product of that project, that can be used to predict values of a result metric. Researchers have, over the last decade, been researching into whether there are important measurable features of specifications, designs or program code that can be used to predict future activities in a software project.

The further into a project a predictor metric is capable of predicting, then the better that metric. For example, if it is possible to extract a metric from a software project during system design, that can predict the amount of resource needed for maintenance, then that metric is very good indeed. It enables the project manager to examine a system architecture during system design, and order his team to redesign if the value is too high. This is a major improvement over discovering unpleasant facts about a system during the maintenance process, when expensive redesign, reprogramming, and retesting would have to take place.

Metrics offer the hard-pressed software project manager a set of tools that promise to transform his way of working. First, as I have described above, it allows more accurate prediction to take place. Second, it allows the project manager to set precise standards. For example, if a detailed design exceeds a particular project value, then either an explanation is required of the staff who transgressed, or the detailed design would have to be reworked. Third, it enables the project manager to appraise the work of staff. Finally, it might form the basis for the scientific appraisal of development methods. A week never goes by without another software development technique being announced. Always, these techniques are claimed to lower programming effort and produce systems that are trivial to maintain. Metrics such as system design metrics should enable the software community to judge these competing claims.

The history of product metrics is a colourful one. Its roots lie in the late 1960s, when Maurice Halstead, a Professor of Computer Science at Purdue University in the United States, developed the theory that there are general laws that govern software systems, and that these laws enable developers to predict important features of a system, such as testability.[2] Halstead used an intoxicating mixture of thermodynamics, cognitive psychology, computer science, and information theory to produce the subject he called software science.

Even though much of Halstead's work is extremely difficult to understand, many of his ideas were quite seductive. The most important one was that, by measuring easily extracted properties of a program, such as the number of identifiers and the number of operators, a developer could could obtain quantitative metrics of testability and readability, and a prediction of the number of residual errors remaining in a system after being tested. Because of the ease with which Halstead's metrics could be extracted, his ideas were taken up by large numbers of researchers in the United States; the collective term used to describe such work was software science Certainly, in the 1970s virtually every American software engineering conference contained a paper on software science.[3]

During the early 1970s, when Halstead's influence was at its peak, another American researcher, Thomas McCabe,[4] devised a different metric that was based on the flow of control inside a program. A computer program or a subroutine can be represented by a mathematical structure known as a directed graph. The example that I gave in Chapter 1 is reproduced as Figure 3.1.

Such a graph consists of a series of points and lines joining these points. Each point, for example 5 or 6, represents a decision in the software, while a line such as j shows the direction that execution of the software would take in response to that decision.

McCabe stated that the more complex a graph, i.e. the more it has lines crossing and the greater the number of decisions, the poorer the software

represented by that graph. His ideas were rooted in common sense: a program
represented by a complex graph contains fairly tortuous logic, and many more
paths than a simple graph. Hence, it it less readable and requires a lot more
testing. McCabe backed up his conjecture with a survey of the modules at his
installation. He discovered that those that had the highest graph complexity were
so complex that they were regarded as no-go areas for modification.

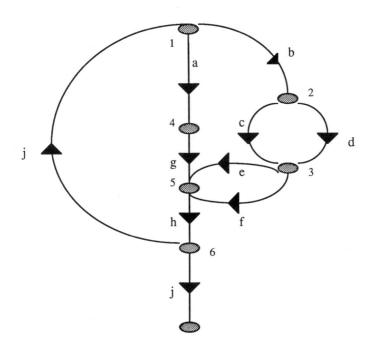

**Figure 3.1.** The directed graph of a program fragment.

McCabe's research also attracted a large number of researchers. They carried
out their work in two areas. First, by attempting to validate McCabe's work
using experiments in which factors such as the error rate of a program were
compared to the complexity of the program. Second, in refining McCabe's
metric in order to improve it. Indeed, in the 1970s you were not a respectable
American academic if you hadn't invented at least one new graph complexity
metric. The major improvements on McCabe's metric were motivated by
criticisms that it didn't measure all the aspects of the complexity of a module or
program. For example, it  didn't measure the use of data inside a module or
program.

Both McCabe's and Halstead's work are now mature; so mature that almost
every book written on software engineering in the last ten years has quoted them
as authoritative sources. However, recent British work suggests that all is not

well with Halstead's metric in particular. In order to explain this criticism I must deviate slightly and briefly describe how to evaluate a metric. When I read a paper announcing a new metric I judge it using a number of criteria. Two of the most important are its intuitive correctness and the degree of validation that it has received. If a metric corresponds to what I regard as important properties of a design or a program, which reflect the difficulty of designing or programming, then that metric has passed its first major test. If the metric has been validated in a number of experiments with a realistic number of subjects or, even better, has been validated on real software projects, then it has passed its second major test. The third major test is how useful that metric is. A metric that can only be extracted late in a software project, say during programming, is not very useful. By that time the developer will have irrevocably committed a large amount of resource

Halstead's work has very limited use on a software project. The reason for this is that since it is oriented towards program code, numerical values of software quality are only available late in the software project when many strategic decisions have been made on specification and system design.

A second criticism concerns the first criterion stated above. The vast majority of papers on software science do not correspond to the measurement of factors that one intuitively feels can be used to judge the difficulty of activities such as programming and testing.

However, even more damaging than these two criticisms is a series of studies carried out on the statistical significance of the validations of the metrics. Until fairly recently, there seemed to be large corpus of statistical work that supported Halstead's work. Many researchers had measured the various software science metrics, and found a relatively high correlation between them and process metrics such as the time to test a module or the time to understand a module. Recently, two researchers at the British Company STC, Peter Hamer and Gillian Frewin,[5] investigated the data which had been generated from a number of classical software science experiments. The conclusion they reached was that the experimental methods used were invalid, and the results generated were unable to support any hypotheses that could be of use to the software project manager.

The degree of criticism of Halstead's work, together with the limited use that can be made of both software science and graph metrics, has persuaded researchers into the potentially more interesting area of system design metrics. This research is much more potentially rewarding than that based on code metrics. This is because the system design is one of the major items in the software project, and has a major influence on the resources needed for activities such as detailed design, programming, unit testing, integration testing, and acceptance testing.

Much of the present work on system design complexity and associated metrics has been inspired by the British architect Christopher Alexander. In the early 1960s Alexander published a book, *Notes on the Synthesis of Form*,[6] that became a seminal work for architects and designers. The thesis he put forward was that a good design, be it the design of an electric shaver or a building, had the property that its parts were independent from each other; and that each component of a good design had few connections with other components. Alexander finished his book with a description of how the principles were used to describe the design of an Indian village.

The application of this thesis to hardware is easy to see: if a computer can be partitioned into a number of hardware modules, then maintenance is easy to carry out; all is required is for the engineer to detect which hardware module is malfunctioning and replace it, without needing to disturb the rest of the computer.

However, Alexander's ideas have application to software as well. If a software system can be designed so that each of its modules is in isolation to the others, then a number of advantages accrue. First, maintaining a system becomes easier: the maintenance programmer does not have to keep details of other modules in his head when carrying out amendments. Second, testing becomes easier, since the tester does not have to worry about the system environment when generating test data. Third, programming becomes easier, because the programmer can localize his thoughts to one chunk of software.

The last five years have seen impressive research results that confirm Alexander's work. Two of the most thorough studies have been carried out at the University of Iowa and Bell Laboratories. In Chapter 1, I described how Sally Henry and Denis Kafura at Iowa had shown that the isolation of program units in the UNIX operating system has a major effect on the number of errors created during detailed design and coding. The metric they employed quantified the isolation of UNIX modules in terms of the information flow between modules. They found a direct correlation between their metric and the maintenance effort for each module in the UNIX system.

In what was probably the largest study of system design metrics yet, Doug Troy and Stuart Zweben[7] of Bell Laboratories examined 21 different metrics. They correlated the values of these metrics for modules against the number of errors in the modules that were discovered during integration and system testing. They found that the best metrics were those that measured the independence of a module from other modules in a system. This confirmed Christopher Alexander's original thesis.

The findings of Kafura and Henry, and Troy and Zweben, have been backed up by a number of further studies that have provided confirmatory evidence. System design metrics seem to pass all the criteria that I described earlier: first, on the basis of empirical validation, it seems that they provide a good indication of software quality, and can predict the extent of future activities such as integration testing and maintenance; second, on the grounds of intuition they match the practice of good system designers; third, coming early in the software project, they can provide the manager with a high degree of prediction. It is this ascendancy of system design metrics that is stimulating some of the most exciting current research in software engineering. There are two facets to this research: the first is concerned with the dynamics of large software systems, the second lies on the frontiers of artificial intelligence research.

The study of the dynamics of software systems has achieved major importance in the last ten years because of major problems with system maintenance. As much as 60% of project resource is now expended in chasing and rectifying errors, adding new functions to a system, and adapting a system to new hardware and software environments. However, as more and more modifications are carried out to a system, its structure degrades and its entropy increases. The reason for this is twofold: first, staff unfamiliar with a software system are usually assigned to its maintenance; second, relatively low-grade staff are also employed in this activity. What happens then is that a software system, when released, starts off with a clean architecture. During maintenance, errors are discovered and new requirements arise, and random hacks are made to the system. This results in interfaces between modules becoming more complex and the logic inside each module becoming more tortuous. What happens is a progressive rusting of the software system which adversely affects further maintenance effort: as the system rusts, further change becomes more difficult and consumes more resource.[8]

Many software managers in charge of maintenance have described to me how modifying a system is relatively easy during the initial stages of maintenance. However, as time goes by, more and more effort is required, even for straightforward change; this leads to the point at which so much effort is expended for a very marginal gain in system value, that the software becomes obsolete.

Studies of large systems such as IBM's OS/360 have shown that a system can rust very quickly. In order to cope with this, researchers are beginning to model the dynamics of software systems using concepts of independence based on system design metrics. Probably the most thorough research in this area was recently carried out by Jim Collefello and Stephen Yau at Northwestern University in the United States.[9]

They modelled a software system by means of a mathematical, two-dimensional structure known as a matrix. An entry in this matrix represents the probability that a change in one module of the system will lead to a change in any module that is connected to it. This clearly measures the quality of a design in terms of the effect of change during maintenance. A good design is one in which a change can be made to a module without its affecting too many other modules. An example of such a matrix is shown in Figure 3.2.

It describes a software system with six modules: $A, B, C, D, E$, and $F$. Each entry in the matrix represents the probability that a change in one module will have on another. The highest probability is 1, which means that a change is certain. The lowest probability is zero which means that there is no certainty of change. The second entry in the first row shows that if there were a change to module $A$ then there would be a finite probability of 0.1 of a change occurring to module $B$. Notice that the diagonal of the matrix consists of certainties. The reason for this is straightforward: if a module is changed then it is certain it is changed.

$$
\begin{array}{c}
\begin{array}{cccccc}
A & B & C & D & E & F
\end{array} \\
\left[
\begin{array}{cccccc}
1.0 & 0.1 & 0.1 & 0.2 & 0.2 & 0.3 \\
0.0 & 1.0 & 0.1 & 0.0 & 0.0 & 0.0 \\
0.1 & 0.2 & 1.0 & 0.1 & 0.1 & 0.0 \\
0.0 & 0.0 & 0.0 & 1.0 & 0.0 & 0.4 \\
0.0 & 0.2 & 0.2 & 0.1 & 1.0 & 0.0 \\
0.0 & 0.0 & 0.0 & 0.5 & 0.1 & 1.0
\end{array}
\right]
\begin{array}{c}
A \\ B \\ C \\ D \\ E \\ F
\end{array}
\end{array}
$$

**Figure 3.2.** Probability matrix for a system containing six modules.

There are also second-order effects embodied in the matrix. For example, if a change occurs to module $A$ then there is a probability of 0.3 that there will be a change to module $F$. However, if there is a change to module F then there is a probability of 0.5 that there will be a change to module $D$. Hence there will be a probability of 0.15 (0.3*0.5) that a change in module $A$ will affect module $D$. There are also third-, fourth-, fifth-, $n$th-order effects embodied in the matrix. For example, a third-order effect is exemplified by the fact that a change to a module affects another module that, in turn affects a further module that, again affects a further module.

In essence the matrix measures the ripple affect that might occur in a software system during maintenance, where a change to a module might ripple its way into other modules. In fact you can use relatively simple algebra to show that, after a certain point, a system described by such a matrix becomes unstable: a change to a module is amplified so much throughout the system that inordinate resources are consumed in implementing that change.

The probabilities are derived by using essentially the same methods that Kafura and Henry employ. Given this matrix, programs can be written that process a system design or the program code of a system, and enable the project manager to judge how much his system has rusted. The major use of such a tool is to enable the project manager to decide when to lower entropy by cleaning up a system: carrying out activities such as making interfaces simpler, recoding complex modules, and rewriting system documentation.

The second area of research is concerned with automatic software design. Design as a discipline has already been recognized as a process of synthesizing alternatives and selecting a 'best' design from these alternatives. Unfortunately, until results emerged from recent metrics work, software designers have had few objective measures of what 'best' means. However, the recent upsurge in system design metrics work has given the software developer the ability to evaluate and discard potential designs.

The logical extension to this is for the computer to carry out this work using techniques from artificial intelligence. Already, teams have prototype systems for this in existence. At Honeywell's System and Research Centre at Minneapolis, developers have devised a module interconnection language that describes how a system is built up from components. They then use artificial intelligence techniques to search for a design that has the highest metric value. Similar research is being carried out at the Open University,[10] where researchers represent the structure of a software system using an artificial-intelligence-based data structure known as an AND/OR graph. An example of such a graph is shown in Figure 3.3.

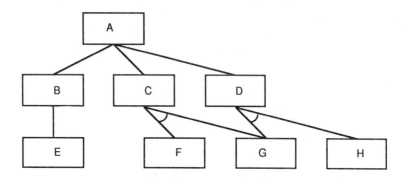

**Figure 3.3**. An example of an AND/OR graph used in software design.

Each box in the AND/OR graph represents a module. In the graph of Figure 3.3 there are eight modules. A line joining one module to another indicates that the top-most module uses the bottom module in carrying out some computation. An arc between lines indicates that the designer has to use both the modules to which the lines are attached in his design. No arc indicates that the designer has a choice of modules. For example, in the above design the designer has to use module A in his design, he has the choice between using modules B, C, or D. If he chooses B then he has to use module E, if he chooses module C then he has to use both modules F and G; similarly, if he uses D he has to use modules G and H. The graph represents a number of possible designs (they are ABE, ACFG, ADGH) and essentially represents a solution space of possible designs.This AND/OR graph is typed into a software tool that then searches for a design with the highest metric value. The research at the Open University differs from the Honeywell research in that a combination of operations research and artificial intelligence is used. However, it is driven by the same philosophy: that system design metrics enable the developer to synthesize a good design, which minimizes resource expenditure during subsequent phases of the software project.

Metrics seem to have a healthy future. In the past they have been held back because of the inability of experimenters to collect them automatically. If metrics are going to be of any use at all then they are going have to be extracted automatically from the products and processes of the software project. It is no good asking staff to calculate them and fill in myriads of forms: calculating metrics is a time-consuming and error-prone activity. This is probably the reason why code metrics, such as those that originate from software science, have been popular: every computer installation keeps program code on on-line files. It is relatively trivial to process such files to extract metrics from them.

In the past it has been much more difficult to extract metrics for design and specification, because the notations used were not machine processable, and only existed on sheets of paper. Happily, this will probably change over the next decade. There is now a new breed of computer program that is similar to the computer-aided design tools used in such areas as ship building and construction engineering. Such tools store and display design notations and, hence, are capable of being modified to extract metrics' values.

Another reason for my optimism about metrics is connected with the rise of the expert system which I detail elsewhere in this book. Expert systems are programs that store the knowledge of an expert in a particular narrow domain. For example, expert systems have now been built that carry out tasks such as the diagnosis of soya bean disease or providing advice on tax matters. These expert systems have been at their most successful where the application domain has been numeric in nature; for example, when they process numerical values of patient temperature, depth of rock formations, the current value of the stock exchange, and line voltages in a telephone exchange. If expert systems are to be used successfully in software engineering then they will have to process exact data; some of that data will arise from metrics.

The last ten years have seen major changes in research and development in metrics. On the surface much of this can be seen as defeats for the proponents of metrics. However, what is happening is only a reflection of what is happening generally to software engineering: that the emphasis in research and development is moving away from activities that are now regarded as trivial, for example, programming, towards the activities, such as design, that determine how untroubled a project manager's life will be.

# References

1.  An excellent account of metrics, and how they might be used in a software project, is contained in: *Controlling Software Projects*, T. de Marco, New York: Yourdon Press. 1982.

2.   The kernel of Halstead's ideas can be found in the book: *Elements of Software Science*, M. H. Halstead, New York: Elsevier - North Holland. 1977.

3.   A book that contains a balanced account of Halstead's work, together with a large number of references to Halstead metric papers is: *Software Engineering Metrics and Models*, S. D. Conte, H. E. Dunsmore, and V. Y. Shen, Menlo Park, Calif: Benjamin Cummings. 1986.

4.   The basis of this work can be found in the paper: A Complexity Measure, T. J. McCabe, *IEEE Transactions on Software Engineering*, **2**, 12. 1976.

5.   Their dissection of the Software Science approach can be found in the paper: M. H. Halstead's Software Science — A Critical Examination, G. Frewin and P. Hamer, *Proceedings 6th International Conference on Software Engineering*. Tokyo, 1982.

6.   *Notes on the Synthesis of Form*, C. Alexander, Cambridge, Mass: Harvard University Press. 1965

7.   Measuring the Quality of Structured Designs, D. A.Troy and S. H. Zweben, *Journal of Systems and Software*, **2**. 1981.

8.   A good description of structural degradation can be found in: Programs Cities and Students — Limits to Growth?, M. M. Lehman, in *Programming Methodology*, D. Gries (Ed.), New York: Springer Verlag. 1978.

9.   A good example of Yau and Collefello's work is: Ripple Effect Analysis of Software Maintenance, S. S. Yau and J. S. Collofello, *Proceedings COMPSAC 78*. 1978.

10.  This particular application of artificial intelligence technology is described in: The Application of Artificial Tools and Techniques in Software Engineering, in *Software Engineering: the Crucial Decade*, London: Peter Peregrinus. 1986.

# 4

# Mathematics and the new software puritans

At 3.10 p.m. on the 30 July 1914, Winston Churchill sent the following to the commander in chief of the Mediterranean naval forces.

> Should war break out and England and France engage in it, it now seems probable that Italy will remain neutral and that Greece can be made an ally. Spain will also be friendly and, possibly, an ally. The attitude of Italy is, however, uncertain and it is especially important that your squadron should not be seriously engaged with Austrian ships before we know what Italy will do. Your first task should be to aid the French in the transportation of their African Army, by covering, and, if possible, bringing to action individual fast German ships, particularly *Goeben* who may interfere with that transportation. You will be notified by telegraph when you may consult with the French admiral. Do not at this stage be brought to action against superior forces, except in combination with the French, as part of a general battle. The speed of your squadrons is sufficient to enable you to choose your moment. We shall hope later to reinforce the Mediterranean and you must husband your forces at the outset.

In this chapter I will be looking at the use of mathematics on software projects. By examining the text above I hope to give you a graphical indication of the problems that software engineers face in analysing the natural-language documents that are currently used on software projects. Military communications are meant to be models of clarity. However, even a writer as good as Churchill can exhibit the types of errors that bedevil current software projects.

First, there is quite a large amount of verbosity in the message. The first 67 words could be replaced by

> If England and France go to war, Greece, and perhaps Spain could become allies. Italy will probably remain neutral but, until this is known, avoid major engagements with Austrian ships.

There are also a number of inconsistencies and ambiguities. First, should the British naval forces have brought to action individual slow German ships? The text does not make this clear. Are the British forces only to engage with German ships that are individual, fast, and interfering with French troop transport? What should the fleet have done if they encountered two slow German ships interfering with the French transports? The text starting with the words Do not at this stage, seems to instruct the Commander-in-Chief that he should enter a battle along with the French and conserve his forces. Quite a contradiction!

The telegram heralded one of the most ignominious episodes in British Naval history and was a factor that led to the entry of Turkey into the First World War. This contributed to the eventual demise of the Ottoman Empire and, together with the increasing importance of oil supplies in the Middle East, led to the major problems that have tragically unfolded in Israel, the Lebanon, and Egypt.[1]

Thus, one small piece of text, written in natural language, played a major part in Middle East history. While nobody would sensibly claim that the texts used in a software project would have such global consequence, nevertheless, misunderstanding of natural language has led, at best, to major budget overspends and, at worst, to cancellation, and, in a local context, can cause as many problems as Churchill's original telegram caused to the British forces in the Mediterranean.

The first document that a software developer is given is the customer statement of requirements. This is an expression, expressed in customer terms, of what he requires from a software system. I have seen statements of requirements scribbled down on sheets of rough paper and, also, well-prepared statements, printed using up-to-date laser equipment, with flashy covers and with company logos liberally scattered throughout the text; but no matter how such statements are prepared and presented, they suffer from the same problems that Churchill's telegram suffered from. First, they are ambiguous. A typical sentence that might occur in such a document is:

The operator identity consists of the operator name and his password; the password consists of six digits. It should be displayed on the security screen and deposited in the login file when an operator first starts to use the system.

Does the word 'it' refer to the password or the operator identity? A second problem with statements of requirements is that they are usually vague. A typical example of vagueness that I often encounter is the sentence: 'The computer system should be user-friendly'. This is a platitude; it is difficult to understand what is required when you encounter it. Does it mean that when a system is started up should it display a message: 'Hi I'm Desmond your friendly software system', or what? Normally when a customer writes down such a statement he usually requires facilities such as a HELP command, which, when activated, gives the user an explanation of some of the facilities of the system.

A statement of requirements will also be contradictory. For example, on one page the user may ask for data to be stored for six months on the computer system and, on another page, specify that the computer to be purchased contains enough storage for only a month of data.

Another serious error that occurs is incompleteness. The fragment of a statement of requirements for a system to monitor the operation of a chemical plant, shown below, contains examples of this.

The system should maintain the hourly pressure values from sensors which are attached to functioning chemical reactors. These values should be stored for the past three months.

A plant operator, when he wishes to find out the average daily pressure value for a specified reactor, for a particular day, types in the word AVERAGE, followed by the day required and the name of the reactor.

There are a number of problems with this. What happens if the operator mis-types the word AVERAGE; what does the system do? How should the operator communicate the day to the system: as figures separated by slashes or as a figure followed by an abbreviated month followed by the year? What happens when the operator mis-types a reactor name? What happens if the operator types in the name of a reactor that is not functioning? The statement of requirements seems to imply that some of the reactors will not be working, perhaps owing to maintenance. What happens when the operator types in the current date? If he types in a request for the average pressure soon after midnight, the value given would not be much help. Should the system tell him this?

A further property of a statement of requirements is that functions, constraints such as response time, and hardware details will all be mixed up together with little organization. Furthermore, some of the statement of requirements will be written at a high level of abstraction, with little explanation, while other requirements will be written in inordinate detail: this is usually an indication that a number of people have been involved in the writing of the statement of requirements.

Statements of requirements will also be naive. This used to manifest itself in customers asking for some part of a system to be implemented in hardware when it could much more easily, and cheaply, be implemented as a software subsystem. Today, with the increased exposure that artificial intelligence has in the media, users now ask for systems well beyond the wildest dreams of the most ardent proponents of that subject.

All the examples above have been somewhat obvious. Statements of requirements suffer from much more subtle and dangerous errors than the ones I have described. Also, other documents in the software project suffer from the same problems. For example, the system specification, if written in natural language, will contain its share of ambiguities, contradictions, and inconsistencies, although, admittedly, there will be a smaller number than in the statement of requirements. However, the smaller number of errors is more than offset by another problem: the size of the system specification. When a software developer amplifies a statement of requirements, and transforms it into a system specification, its size can be increased by a factor of 50 or more. This means that any errors will be much more difficult to detect. It's no use asking the customer to validate a specification: since it occupies many volumes of text, it is a task well beyond the most compute-literate customer.

Documents containing natural language will always contain these errors. It is not the fault of the customer that such errors creep in; anything but the most trivial software system is extremely complex compared with the artefacts produced by more mature disciplines. To ask the customer for a software system to maintain a high level of accuracy over 50 pages of natural language and, likewise, ask the developer to maintain the same level of accuracy, over thousands of pages, is clearly unrealistic. Consequently, software developers are turning to the medium that, since antiquity, has always offered a high degree of precision: mathematics.

Mathematics has for many years been proposed as the ideal medium for software development. The earliest paper in which this proposal was put forward was written in 1967.[2] Originally the reason why mathematics was seen as a solution to programming problems was the unease that a number of computer scientists felt about testing. They were worried that although testing would uncover errors in a program, it was not capable of providing the correct level of confidence that a program was correct.

The first breakthrough in the use of mathematics was achieved by a British computer scientist: Tony Hoare, then at Queens University, Belfast, now Professor of Computation at the University of Oxford. In 1969 Hoare showed that the effect of the various facilities in a programming language could be described by mathematics,[3] the mathematics Hoare used was logic. His work enabled a software developer to construct a program, write down the effect of the program using logic, and demonstrate, by means of the proof methods we all learned in school, that the program matched its description.[4]

This was a seductive idea; it heralded a massive increase in research into methods of proving a program correct. However, researchers soon came up against a barrier: the length of the proofs, for anything but the smallest programs, was quite long. Indeed, many of the proofs were textually longer than the programs that were written and, consequently, were more prone to error than the programs themselves.

In an attempt to overcome this problem, computer scientists at American and British universities attempted to develop software systems that carried out the proofs automatically. Again, this effort was only partially successful. Such proof systems were capable of automating some of the drudgery associated with program proving, but they soon came up against the problem of proofs becoming larger and larger. In fact, the growth of the textual size of a proof seems to be exponential. After a certain program size, even automated systems failed to carry out proofs without spending an inordinate amount of time, or running out of memory. The reason for this is clear: the proof process required seems to be heavily dependent on human intuition. Many of the automatic proof systems that have been built have had to rely on brute-force tactics.[5] These tactics have been so unsubtle that, once a proof system based on these tactics processes anything but a small program, it tends to be in trouble.

Although there are a number of automatic proof systems in existence, their use is in industry is very limited indeed. However, formal methods are still of value to the software developer. One particularly important use is in proving that the kernel of a highly reliable system is correct. There are a number of application areas where a high degree of confidence is required of software; for example, railway signalling, the control of nuclear installations, and the control of advanced, fly-by-wire jet planes. Much of the software for such systems consists of a series of modules that carry out a function and depend on a set of central facilities provided by a kernel, or core, of modules. For example, in a railway signal system the core of the system would provide facilities such as sensing whether a signal was on or off, and changing the state of a signal. A highly reliable system depends so much on this central core of facilities that it is worth using program-proving techniques and automatic proof systems to validate the software.

The comparative failure of program proving led software researchers to play down this aspect of mathematics in software development; in retrospect, this now seems a wise decision, since a much more valuable use for mathematics has emerged during the late eighties. The early 1980s saw a rare agreement between software developers and researchers: that there was a major problem with notations for the front-end of software projects. Many medium and large projects were delivering software that did not meet user's needs and, furthermore, were over-budget and late.

Mathematics seemed the natural medium for specifying systems, and a number of researchers developed notations that could be used for system specification. There is a subtle difference between this use of mathematics and its use in program proving. In program proving, mathematics is used to describe the function of individual programs or modules. In system specification the aim is more ambitious: to describe whole systems. Consequently, the mathematics used for system specification is much richer. As well as using formal logic it employs set theory: the mathematics governing the behaviour of groups of objects. In order to give you a slightly artificial flavour of what it is like to specify a system using mathematics, a diversion is necessary. Examine the statements below:

$$raining \lor cloudy \rightarrow work$$
$$work \rightarrow finish\_book$$
$$finish\_book \rightarrow happy\_publisher$$

They are written in classical logic, and are known as propositions. The symbol $\lor$ stands for *or* the symbol $\rightarrow$ is used for implication: if the left-hand side of the $\rightarrow$ symbol is true then the right-hand side is true. The word *raining* stands for the phrase *it is raining*, the word *cloudy* stands for the phrase *it is cloudy*, the word *work* stands for the phrase *I shall work*, the word *finish_book* means *I shall finish this book* and, finally, the word *happy_publisher* stands for *my publisher will be happy*.

Thus, the first statement can be read in English as: if it is raining or cloudy, then I will work. From the three propositions I can demonstrate that if it is raining my publisher will be happy. The first proposition states that if it is raining or cloudy then I will work. Clearly, if I assume that it is raining then I will work. The second proposition states that if I work then I will finish this book. Since it has been established by the first proposition that I will work, then from the second proposition, I will finish this book. The third proposition states that if I finish this book my publisher will be happy. Since I have established that I will finish the book, the third proposition tells me that my publisher will be happy. Thus, from the fact that it is raining I have established that my publisher will be happy. Mathematicians say that: *my publisher is happy*, is a valid consequence of the fact that it is raining.

Now let us change the extract above slightly

$$valve1\_open \lor valve2\_open \rightarrow loading\_state$$
$$loading\_state \rightarrow temperature\_low$$
$$temperature\_low \rightarrow low\_temp\_screen$$

All that I have done is to substitute different words for those in the first extract. It now becomes a mathematical specification of a monitoring system for a chemical plant. The first proposition states that if *valve1* is open or *valve2* is open then the reactor is in a loading state: chemicals are being poured into it. The second proposition states that if the reactor is in a loading state then its temperature is low. The third proposition states that if its temperature is low then a low temperature warning screen is displayed on the operator's console.

Using the same techniques as used previously, I can then demonstrate that, if *valve1* is open then a low temperature screen is displayed on the operator's console. Now the example I gave above is artificial: it uses only classical logic.[6] For real specifications a much richer variety of mathematics should be used. It is also artificial because it is small. A real specification would occupy hundreds, if not thousands, of propositions. Nevertheless, it gives a good idea of what using mathematics entails.

First, the developer examines the customer statement of requirements; he then constructs a system specification in some mathematical notation. This is then validated by asking the user questions, and demonstrating formally that the answer given by the user can be deduced from the specification. For example, the question, 'If *valve2* is open then does that mean a low temperature screen is displayed on the operator's console?' is one question that would be asked of the customer for the monitoring system shown above.

A number of researchers have taken the idea of using mathematics further. What they do is to first define a system in terms of mathematical structures, and then gradually transform this description into further mathematical structures that reflect the storage facilities available in today's programming languages. At each stage they have to prove formally that the transformation is correct.

In 1985 the British Department of Trade and Industry announced its strategy for beating off the Japanese challenge in information technology. The strategy was known as the Alvey Programme, named after the chairman of the original working party whose report lead to the establishment of the programme.

When the objectives of the Alvey Programme were published, one of the surprising areas for further development in the software engineering programme was formal methods of software development: the use of mathematics for specifying and designing large, complex systems. Many felt that the idea that software staff should use mathematics in their day-to-day work was over-academic, unrealistic, and doomed to failure. I was certainly surprised, as it represented a discrete jump in the United Kingdom's approach to software development.

At the time of writing this book (1988) has that view been vindicated? Recently I visited a wide variety of software developers, both here and in the United States, who are currently using formal methods. The reason for my visit was that I was involved in the making of a BBC film looking at formal methods in the software industry. The results of the research that I carried out were quite surprising.

My first visit was to IBM's Scientific Laboratories at Hursley Park. The team, who use mathematics for software development, are employing a notation known as Z in specifying a transaction-processing system CICS.[8] This system is one of IBM's most successful products. However, it now suffers from its success. Users have continually demanded changes to enhance the software and it has also had to adapt to new hardware and software systems. This meant that its structure was degraded to the point where IBM decided to re-implement it. The team carrying out the re-implementation started by specifying the system using Z.

Team members who were previously very sceptical told me of the advantages that accrued from the process. First, since mathematics is precise it enabled teams to communicate in an unambiguous way, and eliminated the serious interface errors that occur in large projects. Second, IBM have found that the review process has been radically transformed.

Reviews are a highly effective way of discovering errors in project documents or in software. It consists of a meeting between a number of project personnel in which a document or program is examined in minute detail and errors are discovered. It is the formalization of the experience of many software staff who, after many hours of staring at a program in order to discover an error, have that error discovered by a colleague who looks at the offending program for a few seconds. IBM were the pioneers in carrying out peer-group reviews of requirements documents and designs, and have found it an effective means of validating a software system. However, when you are dealing with a notation such as natural language, major problems are encountered. Often a group of reviewers will become mesmerized by prose and convince themselves of the same interpretation of a piece of text when, in fact, each will have wildly differing interpretations.

Another problem with reviews involving natural language is that a good speaker can, just by force of personality and arm waving, convince his fellow reviewers that a software document is correct even when there are glaring errors in it. The IBM developers that I met stressed that because the specification notation was based on mathematics any doubts could be resolved by carrying out some mathematics.

I next visited Marconi Under Water Weapons Division at Croxley. Here software developers are using a formal method known as Jackson System Design (JSD) to produce simulation and guidance software for the Spearfish intelligent torpedo. JSD is a popular technique used in developing problems that have a strong time dimension: where there is a high degree of concurrency, with a large number of tasks being executed at the same time.[9] It relies heavily on graphic notations, but is based on an area of mathematics concerned with the study of objects known as regular expressions.

JSD was used because its graphic notation was well-suited for liaising with customers and with non-software developmental staff. After employing this formal method, productivity at Marconi was increased by 250% and integration testing time was reduced from 20 weeks to 4 weeks. These are startling figures, because the software development methods previously employed at Marconi were based on respectable structured design and programming techniques.

One of the most surprising users of formal methods that I found was Merlin Geophysical, a geological exploration company. Merlin are in the business of providing processed data to customers such as oil companies. They have the problem of maintaining something like 400 000 lines of FORTRAN code. Normally, a developer who has to maintain this size of scientific package has to commit 60–70% of its resources to maintenance. By using formal methods of software development Merlin have managed to reduce this figure to 10%. This has led to increased staff morale, since it leaves their programmers free to carry out the enjoyable task of creating new code, rather than chasing up errors in existing code.

A recent user of formal methods is Praxis PLC. Probably one of the most innovative software houses in this country. One of the major projects undertaken by Praxis, and funded by the European community, was to define the interfaces to a software system known as the Portable Common Tools Environment (PCTE). Praxis chose a formal method known as VDM, which is based on a technique that was used at the IBM Vienna Laboratories for defining programming languages such as PL/I. They chose VDM because there is a requirement to unambiguously define interfaces to the PCTE. Because there is a European dimension to this project Praxis felt that mathematics was required to communicate with all potential European users of the PCTE. They felt that this would be much more practical than producing a number of poorly translated versions of a flawed natural-language document

A number of surprising points emerged from my survey. First, developers have strong views about using mathematics. There are companies that use formal methods, are very enthusiastic about them, and can demonstrate clear productivity gains that, in some cases, are massive; then there are companies that do not use formal methods, have never considered formal methods, and don't envisage ever using formal methods. These are extremes and, in an albeit impressionistic survey, I did not find any companies which lay between these extremes.

Another strong impression that I gained was the almost obsessive concern by all the developers about the user. Now this really is surprising. The critics of mathematics on software projects have long used the inability of customers to understand mathematics as a stick to beat its proponents. The companies that I encountered had a number of effective solutions to this problem.

IBM Hursley and Praxis believed the best way to approach the problems was by constructing a new type of user manual. In this manual, system facilities would be described in both mathematics and natural language. The developer would derive the mathematics first, and then use it to transliterate a clear specification in natural language. The user of such a manual would normally consult the natural language part. However, if there was any doubt about a facility then the user would call on his resident mathematics guru who would provide an exact explanation.

Marconi approached the problem of user participation by adopting JSD because it employs a friendly graphical notation that represents the acceptable face of the underlying mathematics. In fact, this mirrors much of what is common practice in many other branches of engineering. For example, electrical engineers who design microwave devices do not normally use mathematics in their design. What they do is to use a circular graphical chart known as a Smith chart to calculate quantities such as impedance.

Finally, a number of developers were keen to use prototyping in order to involve the users in development. The technology is now available: a number of universities, for example Stirling University and the Open University, have now developed some very effective tools for taking a mathematical specification and animating it for the user. Praxis are hoping to use prototyping on their PCTE project, while, at British Telecom, software developers are actually translating formal specifications expressed in VDM into the programming language Prolog and producing prototypes extremely quickly.

One benefit that was stressed, time and time again, was that using mathematics freed the developer from a potentially destructive emotional attachment to his software. Since software development using mathematics consists of a series of almost mechanical steps, then, when an error occurs it is an error in manipulation. Consequently, the perpetrator usually feels the minor irritation that would be experienced when, say, mis-typing a character on a keyboard. Designers who use techniques in which systems are dredged from the depths of their soul tend to suffer trauma when an error is discovered.

The possible future for software developers who fail to use formal methods of software development was graphically described to me by John Coplin, Director of Design at Rolls Royce, who was a contributor to the Government ACARD report on Information Technology. He described development practice on aero-engine projects in the 1950s and 1960s. Specification and design were then carried out only in a relatively informal way. However, a large amount of resources was devoted to checking an engine in a test shed. The engine would be driven to full power; this would normally result in a component failure. The component would then be strengthened and the test restarted. This time another component would fail. This process was continued until no component failure occurred.

Coplin explained to me that increased competition in the aero-engine business led to this wasteful practice being abandoned and much more effort being put into analysis and design, using mathematics. His first description uncannily mirrored the current ways we develop software: for example, for 'component failure' read 'bug' and for 'component being strengthened' read 'program modification'. Undoubtedly, competition will hot up in the software world; it may well be that it will be those companies that adopt the software analogue of what Rolls Royce do now, and adopt mathematics, that will survive.

These then are the positive aspects of using mathematics in software development: it can be used to communicate clearly between a number of users and members of development teams; it provides an effective medium for prototyping; it frees the software developer from a potentially dangerous, emotional involvement with his software; and it provides a medium for specification where no erroneous interpretations are possible.

Formal methods of software development are currently the topic of hot debate and controversy in Europe. The critics of employing mathematics on a software project often accuse the proponents of formal methods of being intellectual puritans, and of stifling all the creativity in the software development process.

There is a very small element of truth in the reference to puritanism. The proponents of formal methods are, like the Roundheads, correct but boring: their opponents, like the Cavaliers, are wrong but romantic. There is an enjoyment in developing a program, and then hunting for errors by continually running the program with test data. To eliminate a set of errors and see your program working in front of your eyes is akin to the pleasure that a crossword expert gets when solving a particularly cryptic clue. It is also similar to the pleasure that experimental scientists feel when they obtain good results from experiments that back up their hypotheses. Unfortunately, commercial software development is a serious and expensive process, and to regard it as similar to experimental science, as we have done in the past, will, at best, lead to tears, and, at worst, lead a continuation of the poor reputation that software developers have had in the past.

It is fair to point out that there are a number of major barriers to the wide-scale adoption of mathematics in the software industry. These are explored in the next chapter, which describes one of the most startlingly successful uses of mathematics on a software project that I know of.

# References

1.  An excellent account of the subsequent episodes in this piece of naval history can be found in: *The Ship that Changed the World*, D. van der Vat, London, U.K.: Collins. 1985.

2.  Assigning Meanings to Programs, R. Floyd, *Proceedings Symposium on Applied Mathematics*, **19**. Providence, R.I.: American Mathematical Society. 1967.

3.  An Axiomatic Basis of Computer Programming, C. A. R. Hoare, *Communications of the ACM*, **12**, 10. 1969.

4.  The best description of this process is contained in the book: *Proving Programs Correct*, R. Anderson, New York: John Wiley. 1979.

5.  A good description of what is probably the best system, GYPSY, is: Mechanical Proofs about Computer Programs, D. I. Good, in *Mathematical Logic and Programming Languages*, Englewood Cliffs: N.J.: Prentice-Hall. 1985.

6.  For an example of a richer mathematical notation used for specification, see the collection of papers: *Specification Case Studies*, I. J. Hayes (Ed.), Englewood Cliffs, N.J.: Prentice-Hall. 1986.

7.  A technique based on this idea is described in: *Systematic Software Development Using VDM*, C. B. Jones, Englewood Cliffs, N.J.: Prentice-Hall. 1986.

8.  A good description of the training required to introduce Z into Hursley is contained in: Teaching Formal Specification Methods in an Industrial Environment, *Proceedings Software Engineering 86*, London: Peter Peregrinus. 1986.

9.  A good tutorial on JSD is in: An Overview of JSD, J. Cameron, *IEEE Transactions on Software Engineering*, **12**, 2. 1986.

# 5

# The cleanest room in Bethesda

If you visit a semiconductor plant you will be struck by a fanatical approach to cleanliness: the most expensive air conditioning is used, high-quality filters and air locks will have been installed, and fabrication equipment will be regularly checked in minute detail. Large numbers of staff are employed, just to ensure that no speck of dust is allowed to enter the clean rooms where semiconductor fabrication takes place. The reason for this is clear: just one impurity of a few microns would ruin an integrated circuit.

This same fanatical approach to cleanliness is now being adopted by software developers in order to remove the software analogue of specks of dust: program bugs; one of these developers is IBM. The IBM Federal Systems Division Building at Bethesda is a typical IBM building: tinted glass, the purest air conditioning you can find in Maryland, and no litter. It seems only apposite that they have adopted the clean-room approach to software development. Developers at FSD regard any bug in a piece of software as seriously as a speck of dust in a VLSI circuit.

Its quite easy to dismiss this as advertising hype. We can all imagine the IBM marketing division sitting down examining and rejecting advertising options. Sixth-generation languages? No, it's too early. Revamping an old range of computers with different packaging? No, all our competitors are doing that, we need something special. Artificial intelligence tools? It sounds promising; however, the market's not ripe for that one. What about bug-free software? What a concept! No more boring error report forms to fill in; no more interminable phone calls from irate customers with little sense of humour and the inability to describe simple errors. Perhaps we could run a whole advertising campaign, we could use those guys from Ghost Busters in our TV adverts. Perhaps they could kill off some bugs ...

The IBM approach to developing clean-room software is a serious one that originates from some major concerns about software quality. During the development process software is usually tested very heavily. This normally discovers many programming errors. However, testing can also discover errors that have been committed early in a project. This can be extremely serious for the developer; for example, a specification error detected during programming will almost invariably involve very expensive respecification and redesign. Such errors have even caused the cancellation of major projects.

What is becoming increasingly clear is that no matter how efficient a developer's testing strategy, it always seems to leave a number of residual errors in a product long after it has been shipped. These are normally discovered by the customer during use, and often requires a number of releases of the software. Each release will normally clear up all the discovered errors. Unfortunately, the correction of errors often introduces further errors that, invariably, leads to further releases.

Testing technology has improved to the extent that the norm of thousands of undiscovered errors in a medium-size system no longer occurs. However, it is still very common to discover many hundreds of errors in the release of a software system.

Although, on first sight, this seems an improvement, it still has serious repercussions on software quality. This was borne out by a recent American Government study that showed that, because of errors, 47% of the software systems from nine sample projects were delivered but never used by the customer and that 29% were paid for but never delivered.

To overcome this serious problem, IBM have taken the term 'software engineering' seriously. They have seen that mathematics is used in other engineering subjects such as civil engineering and electronic engineering, and have applied the same methods and disciplines to software engineering. The IBM team involved in the clean-room experiment employed mathematics as the medium for describing what their system is to do. This mathematical description was then developed into a program via a series of transformations that were mathematically validated at each stage.[1] The validation was checked by a series of peer-group reviews scheduled throughout the project. The team carried out no testing until the very final stages of the project. I'll repeat that sentence: the team carried out no testing until the very final stages of the project. They just added together all the modules they produced and then acceptance-tested the resulting system.

This is completely different from conventional practice. In current projects, testing starts as soon as the first modules of a system are programmed, where each module is unit-tested to check that it meets its design. The system is then gradually built up, module by module, until the whole system has been assembled. Each time that a module is added, further testing is carried out. This is known as integration testing; its main objective is to test that the interface between the added module and the rest of the system is correct, although it often traps errors that should have been picked up during unit testing.

The IBM teams dispensed with this testing, which can take up to 30% of project resource. If you think about it, this was quite a brave thing to do. It ensured that the software product was not visible until very late in a project. In a conventional project you can get a rough idea that you are on the right track during integration testing when the system unfolds before your very eyes. The IBM team waited for the very last moment before running their system.

What was also startling about the project was the test method used to exercise the system. In a normal project the system and acceptance tests are contained in a bulky document called the acceptance test specification. Each test is described in minute detail, together with the criteria used to judge its success. Constructing this document is a major task; it involves the developer examining the system specification, extracting the functions of the system, and deriving a test, or series of tests, that demonstrates to the customer that that each function works. The IBM team ignored this convention and just threw random test data at the system.

There are two advantages to this seemingly haphazard strategy: first, it means that you don't spend too much time constructing the acceptance test specification; second, it enables the development team to predict the error rates that would occur during the operation of the system. One of the nice things about generating random data is that there is a body of theory that you can use to calculate figures such as the error density in a system and its mean time between failure.

The results from IBM were startling.[2] The product that the team developed consisted of 30 000 lines of program code. It was delivered well before the planned release date and the project was substantially under budget. This is quite unusual for a project of this size. However, what was startling about the project was that the number of errors discovered was reduced by an order of magnitude compared with similar projects.

One reason why such exceptional results were obtained could have been the high calibre of staff used on the project. Certainly, IBM have a reputation for hiring only the best. However, the clean-room experiment was recently duplicated with a wide ability range of students at the University of Maryland, and similar results were obtained.[3] Groups of students produced software with a considerable reduction of errors, compared with similar software produced by hardened professionals.

The clean-room approach seems to offer major gains for software developers. However, there is one drawback, and it is a drawback that has serious ramifications for software developers and educators alike. Both the staff at IBM and the students at the University of Maryland had a mathematical background. Although the mathematics that was used was not difficult, it is alien to the majority of staff working on software projects and requires quite a sophisticated level of mathematical expertise from the staff involved.

There are major obstacles to the adoption of mathematics on software projects. Already there are a number of bad signs that these obstacles are preventing real progress. Every seminar on formal methods of software development that I attend usually contains a talk about how mathematics has been used successfully on industrial projects. Unfortunately, it tends to be the same staff who are doing the describing, and the same projects that are being described, as at the talks that I attended the year before.

The second phenomenon that makes me worry about the future use of mathematics in software development is that the projects on which it is applied, certainly the British ones, are heavily subsidized by Government or by EEC money. There do not seem to be too many companies willing to bet hard cash on formal methods of software development.

Another major factor that, at best, will slow up the growth of formal methods is that many British companies tend to skimp on training. One indication of this is that staff in training departments are usually paid less than their counterparts who are involved in development activities. I can still remember turning up to a meeting in 1986, between the manager in charge of training at a major software company and a consultant from the same company. The latter drove up in his company BMW, while the former arrived in a car that was only a few months away from being junked. A further indication of the priority that we put on training is that the longest time most staff are released for training in a year is for the occasional three-day seminar.

The training required to support the methods used at IBM requires a much longer period of study. It normally requires courses lasting weeks, followed by intensive experience on a real project. In many ways one can understand this seemingly negative attitude from industry. Order books are booming and, consequently, customers are prepared to tolerate software that is defective. It just seems a pity that a technique that can bring startling results may not be adopted in the near future for reasons unconnected with its excellence and utility.

Another obstacle to overcome is the major change in organization that will occur if formal methods are adopted: there would be major ramifications for large numbers of staff. These would be so large that there would be considerable opposition. If mathematics were adopted, then the majority of analysts and designers would be highly trained professionals. They would certainly be mathematically very literate. Indeed, in terms of training, job prospects, and status, they would approach their counterparts in other engineering disciplines, where stringent educational and training requirements are insisted on before staff become chartered engineers. If the gains experienced by the clean-room team were realized then there would certainly be a massive increase in productivity, but there would also be an immediate division in software projects between engineers and technicians. The former would carry out the prestigious tasks such as system design, while the latter would carry out the software analogue of soldering: programming and unit testing.

This would be quite a revolution. Software projects are currently staffed by a hotchpotch of staff: high school graduates; university graduates with degrees in non-relevant subjects such as biology and economics; Ph.D. graduates in subjects such as chemistry, who were unable to find jobs in their own field; and an increasing number of computer scientists. Success in the computer industry currently goes to those staff who are good at conventional developmental tasks, rather than those possessing high-grade qualifications. A much more rigid, hierarchical career pattern that would be imposed by the adoption of mathematics as a development medium, would produce the biggest managerial change that software organizations will ever experience and would be resisted all the way by the staff involved.

# References

1.  A description of the development method used by the teams at FSD can be found in the book: *Structured Programming: Theory and Practice*, R. Linger, H. Mills, and B. Witt, Reading, Mass: Addison-Wesley. 1979.

2.  For a good description of the clean-room experiment, and supporting data, see the paper: Software Development Under Statistical Quality Control, in *Software System Design Methods*, Berlin: Springer Verlag. 1986.

3.  Preliminary results from this experiment can be found in: Cleanroom Software Development: An Empirical Evaluation, *University of Maryland Technical Report 1415*. 1985.

# 6

# The rise and slight fall of the expert system

Artificial Intelligence has had a tempestuous history. The study of how computers can mimic human beings has suffered from periods of crisis and periods of boom, the extent of which has not been experienced by any other computer-related discipline.[1] Certainly software engineering has undergone periods of favour and disfavour, but these periods have only been slight deviations.

At the time of writing artificial intelligence is undergoing a boom, the like of which none of its followers could have predicted ten years ago. The reason for this boom is an item of software known as the expert system. Before I look in detail at what expert systems are, and what they do, it is worth briefly describing the early history of artificial intelligence, in particular the research that was undertaken in order to program computers to replicate the problem-solving abilities of the human.

Early work in artificial intelligence in the area of problem solving consisted of developing systems that had the aim of simulating the human problem-solving processes over a large domain of problems. Researchers were not interested whether the problem to be solved was a chess end-game puzzle, the identification of chemical compounds from experimental data, or the understanding of natural language. Many researchers attempted to develop systems that took a domain-independent description of a problem, and attempted to mimic human decision processes in solving that problem.

The performance of such general-purpose strategies was very poor: they could only solve the simplest problems and, moreover, could only solve them very slowly. The preoccupation of researchers with general problem-solving strategies was understandable: if an efficient method of solving any problem could be found, then a major advance would have been made; it would have been such a major advance that it would certainly have qualified the successful researchers for the Nobel prize. It was, therefore, much more exciting than looking at problem solving in one small area. However, even in these early days, the work of one researcher seemed to indicate that more success could be gained in this direction.

In the early sixties an American researcher, Arthur Samuel, had developed a computer program for playing checkers.[2] This program essentially solved problems over a very limited domain: that of checkers. Samuel's program performed extremely well, beating or drawing with some of the top checkers players in America. This was quite an achievement: the program was written for a computer that we, in the 1980s, would regard as hopelessly under-powered. Its success pointed the way towards a major shift in artificial intelligence research. However, the work that can be seen as a turning point in the fortunes of artificial intelligence arose from a problem in organic chemistry.

During the 1960s an American research scientist, Edward Feigenbaum, had become interested in computer reasoning; in particular, he was interested in the interpretation of experimental data by the computer. His work came to fruition in a program called DENDRAL.[3] This piece of software processed readings from a laboratory instrument, known as a mass spectrometer, that bombarded a chemical with high-energy electrons and produced data from which the composition of the chemical could be discovered.

Interpreting mass spectrometer data was a task fitted for experts. It required a large amount of knowledge, and some years experience, to be an efficient user of a mass spectrometer. DENDRAL changed all this. It processed spectrometer data and identified chemicals with an accuracy better than the best human experts. The secret of the program's success was that it limited itself to one small application area. It did not attempt to generalize. It was the first example of an expert system: a program that encapsulated knowledge about a limited domain and performed as well as the human expert.

Even though the success of DENDRAL was startling, there were comparatively few attempts in the 1970s to mimic it. There were two reasons for this: first, researchers were still looking for the big breakthrough by solving problems involving generality and, second, artificial intelligence funding, both in the United States and the United Kingdom, was at a fairly low level — there were certainly more troughs than peaks.

What changed everything was the Japanese. In 1981 the Japanese Government announced a project aimed at producing new, fifth-generation computer technology that was far in advance of the wildest dreams of Western experts. The major components of this technology were logic programming languages and expert systems.[4] In Chapter 15 I describe logic programming languages in more detail; in this chapter I shall concentrate on expert systems.

The effect of the Japanese announcement was immediate. Western governments, having had their car, motor-cycle, and electronics industries severely mauled by the Japanese, perceived an even greater danger: that the Japanese were moving into one of their most profitable and expanding areas, an area where the industrialized Western countries still had the major market share. Immediately a number of national research and development programs were announced. Even if Japan had trumpeted the development of the first wind-powered computer, Western governments would have sunk billions into sail technology!

What particularly shocked observers was the fact that the Japanese were moving into an area where there was little expertise. Very few computer scientists had heard of expert systems[5] or logic programming, and the active research communities in each of these subjects was measured, at best, in tens rather than hundreds or thousands. If the Japanese were right, and expert systems were going to be the software of the future, then they would achieve dominance very quickly, much more quickly than if they had decided to mount a major research programme that extended traditional software and programming languages. Immediately Western governments started pumping money into the areas identified by the Japanese, both in research and development, and in education. Overnight, the expert system assumed a major importance in Western technological planning.

The architecture of a typical expert system is shown in Figure 6.1.

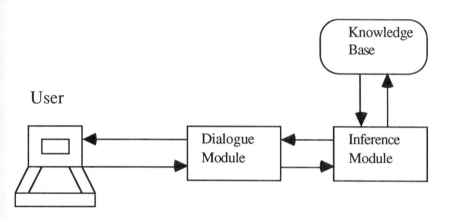

**Figure 6.1**. Schematic architecture of an expert system.

The simplest part of an expert system is the dialogue module. It enables a user to consult with the system. The central core is a knowledge base. This is a store of an expert's knowledge that is used by the expert system. The knowledge is often stored as a series of rules that state that if something is true and something else is true, and so on, then a conclusion can be reached. For example, the rules shown below could be used in an expert system for monitoring a chemical reactor.

IF valve 1 is open AND the temperature is normal AND valve 2 is closed
        THEN the reactor is in wait mode

IF valve 1 is closed AND valve 2 is closed AND temperature is abnormal
        THEN the reactor is in warning mode

IF valve 3 is closed AND the pressure is normal AND valve 2 is open

THEN the reactor is in quiescent mode

IF the reactor is in quiescent mode AND the chemical being produced is ethylene
   THEN a warning message should appear

The rules represent the knowledge of an expert. When the expert system is called upon, it examines all the rules in its knowledge base, and discovers all the known facts about the domain it is being used in, and makes a deduction. Thus, in a system for monitoring chemical reactors, the known facts would be the state of reactor valves, and the temperatures and pressures of reactors. These facts would then be used to make a deduction based on the rules in the knowledge base. For example, if a reactor had valve 2 open and valve 3 closed, and its pressure was normal, and it was producing the chemical ethylene, then a warning message would be displayed on the plant operator's console.

The example of the plant monitoring system that I have used is a highly artificial one. A typical knowledge base consists of hundreds of rules and, in making a deduction, an expert system often has to carry out long and involved processing. The part of the expert system that does this processing is known as the inference module. It essentially carries out automatic deductions. In the case of the chemical plant monitoring expert system it deduced from the state of the valves, the reactor pressure, and the chemical being produced, that a warning was required.

There are a number of stages in developing a commercial expert system. First, a problem domain has to be identified. Expert systems have been successful in a number of application ranges, and for the commercial developer to stray outside these normally courts disaster, unless, of course, the development is being undertaken as part of a research project. The areas where expert systems have been successful are in interpreting and classifying a large amount of data (DENDRAL is a good example of this use); in making diagnoses, such as identifying a limited range of blood diseases; in detecting anomalies such as the breakdown in a telephone circuit; in crisis management, for example, in determining the causes and location of chemical spillage. If the application falls in one of these areas, then the next step in the process is to find an expert in the area that is to be computerized.

Throughout the construction of the expert system, the expert is interrogated and the reasoning processes that he uses are stored in the knowledge base. The interrogation is carried out by a exceptionally skilled member of the developer's team known as a *knowledge engineer*. The dialogue between the knowledge engineer and the expert consists of identifying the data that the expert uses; for example, in a medical diagnosis expert system the expert might use blood chemical data, heart and breathing rates, and blood pressure to help him make a diagnosis. Once these factors are identified the most difficult part of the process of building the knowledge base starts.

The knowledge engineer has to coax out of the expert the reasoning process that takes place each time a conclusion is reached. This is difficult, because most human experts are unaware of the underlying deductions that they make. Often, they make split-second judgements based on a huge amount of accumulated experience. To extract the deduction processes that the expert unconsciously uses needs a huge degree of patience, and requires the knowledge engineer to be quite knowledgeable in the domain being computerized. Because this process consumes a large amount of resource, and because of the need for an extremely highly qualified knowledge engineer, the major bottleneck in the development of expert systems is the knowledge elicitation process.

Once the knowledge base has been developed a sample of cases is processed by the expert system. This sample contains not only normal cases, but also ones that seldom occur. Almost invariably, these unusual cases are highly important, and need to be taken into account. For example, in a chemical monitoring system one such case might represent a series of circumstances that occur very infrequently, but which, if they did occur, would lead to catastrophe. The results are then evaluated both by the expert and also by a panel of outside experts. Almost invariably, the first version of an expert system will have a high degree of failure, and more iterations involving the modification of the knowledge base will be required. Often, this version is no more than a prototype: a feasibility study that shows that data from the application can be used to form computerized deductions.

Once the expert system has been evaluated, the developer has to ensure that the dialogue between the expert system and the user is conducted along the same lines as would be the normal dialogue between the expert and the user. For example, in a medical diagnosis expert system the questions about a particular patient sign such as breathing should all be asked together; the patient should not be asked a question about breathing, followed by a question about headaches, followed by another question about breathing and so on.

The next stage is to ensure that the expert system provides an explanation about its reasoning. This is vitally important in almost all the applications of expert systems. If a computer program is to make diagnoses, or pass judgement, then there must be complete confidence in its operation by its users. For example, a number of expert systems outperform human consultants and, furthermore, are capable of producing conclusions that the consultants would never have thought of. In such cases the expert system should provide an explanation of why it reached its conclusions. Without such an ability a human consultant, faced with an unusual conclusion, that, nevertheless, is correct, will ignore it.

Expert systems have been written in such diverse areas as oil exploration, the diagnosis of infections of the blood, the configuration of computer systems, and molecular genetics. They represent the most commercially viable part of a subject that, for the most part, is still in the research stage. What then are the prospects for expert systems? Unfortunately, they suffer from a number of problems.

The first problem is one of complexity. As soon as the number of rules in an expert system exceeds a certain number, major difficulties occur. First, the process whereby knowledge is extracted from a consultant becomes exceptionally difficult. Second, the performance of the expert system degrades, with the process of consultation by a user becoming slow.

The second problem is that expert systems are too superficial. Their knowledge bases represent only a surface view of how a consultant works. For many applications, rules such as the IF... THEN rules described in this chapter work correctly. However, a human consultant is often called upon to carry out very deep reasoning; for example, when there are competing conclusions that he has to consider. Unfortunately, an expert system is extremely poor at such reasoning.

A third problem is that the interfaces to expert systems are very unnatural. Users have to communicate with expert systems using languages that are highly artificial. Of all the problems currently facing the developers of expert systems this is probably the easiest to overcome. Human–computer interface researchers seem to be solving many of the problems of communicating with the naive user, and I fully expect that very simple interfaces, that allow the user to communicate with expert systems using a restricted subset of natural language, will emerge over the next five years.

Another serious problem with expert systems is that the reasoning process is fixed by the inference module; it cannot be changed. Human consultants use a whole series of methods of reasoning to enable them to reach conclusions, of which deduction based on IF.... THEN rules is just one. The use of only one strategy for reasoning makes the expert system only suitable for a restricted range of applications.

Another major problem is concerned with the structure of expert systems. At the core of an expert system is a knowledge base. For anything but the most superficial applications this knowledge base is extremely complex. The process of building it up tends to be a very hit-or-miss affair, akin to the way an experimental scientist works: the knowledge engineer selects a rule, adds it to the knowledge base, and tries out some sample examples; he then checks the results with a human consultant and if the results are poor then the rule is removed and a new rule is added, and so on. The developer of such an expert system can never give an absolute guarantee that his system is not going to make an error: the nature of the process of building the knowledge base, together with the facts\that the knowledge base is so complicated and that exhaustive testing of an expert system is impossible, means that expert systems, in their present form, will never be used in high-risk applications such as chemical plant monitoring and patient monitoring.

The experience of medical expert system builders in America seems to support this prediction. Almost all the major medical diagnostic expert systems in existence have been developed in America, where litigation over medical malpractice is frequent. Because of the lack of absolute confidence in expert systems, those systems that have been built are normally used for training and are little used in real patient care. It is quite a tricky legal point whom you sue if an expert system delivers wrong conclusions that result in litigation: the knowledge engineer, the company who built the expert system software, the consultant who was questioned during the knowledge elicitation process, the panel of experts who validated the expert system, or the end-user?

A final problem with expert systems involves the nature of the subject of artificial intelligence. Its very name is glamorous. When the Japanese government decided to make expert systems a major component of their information technology strategy, the glamour was increased at least tenfold. From about 1984 onwards you could not pick up a newspaper or science magazine without discovering yet another expert system article. Indeed, I have been guilty of writing a number of them myself. Consequently, customers' expectations of expert systems became quite high: after all, if the Japanese were really interested in them, then surely they would solve many of our computing problems?

Unfortunately, reality has not mirrored the artificially high expectations that were generated in the early 1980s. This is not surprising. Expert system research has progressed as much as any new subject with a limited research community could be expected to progress. This will probably not be good enough, and there will be the inevitable downturn of interest in the area.

My prediction is that over the next decade the initial predictions of the growth in expert system technology will be revised downwards and, because of the problems that I have described above, expert systems will be used more as a decision-support tool rather than as a fully automatic replacement for the human consultant.

A good example of this type of use has occurred in the City of London's financial sector. Data Logic, a major British software company, have developed an impressive expert system for foreign exchange dealing that is currently used in a real application, and is also making large amounts of profit for the customer who uses it.

The major activity of a foreign exchange dealer is the buying and selling of currencies in a number of markets. This is a hyperactive activity where speed is of the essence; where even the suspicion that a currency rate will change by a small fraction of a cent can make the difference between tens of thousands of pounds being lost or gained. There are two ways of analysing any market; be it a currency market, equities market, or commodity market. The first is known as fundamental analysis. It consists of a dealer studying fundamental factors that would affect that market. In an equities market this would involve a dealer buying or selling shares in a company on the basis of factors such as its balance sheet, the current performance of its competitors, and changes in its board of directors.

The second method is known as technical analysis. For example, for a foreign exchange dealer this involves studying the past values of a currency that he is interested in; for an equities dealer this involves studying the past movements of a share price. Dealers who use technical analysis are known as chartists. This is because they draw charts showing past price movements and statistical data such as moving averages. From these charts they can spot a pattern in the past movements of a currency or share.

Clearly, if a currency dealer can spot a pattern developing then there is major potential for large profits. Unfortunately, there are two problems. First, there is the problem of spotting a pattern early enough to make adequate profits. The second problem is that the patterns are usually distorted by noise, which is usually represented by random fluctuations. Hence the patterns that appear are not smooth and require experience and knowledge to discern them.

The Data Logic software recognizes chart patterns and predicts probabilities of trends based on knowledge-based rules. A future version of the system will then present them to trading-room analysts and economists who will then add their own judgements about what will happen and return them to the computer. The computer will then combine their judgements into a prediction. In producing this prediction the computer would use an estimate of how good each economist and analyst has been in the past. Therefore, if an analyst has had a good performance in judging movements in the past the computer takes a lot of notice of him: on the other hand, if an analyst has been consistently wrong in the past, then his estimate is not ignored, but the computer assumes the opposite of his estimate will happen.

The results have been startling. To publicize the system Data Logic challenged a series of city institutions to outperform their software. For three weeks, a team of foreign-exchange dealers was invited to phone assessments of whether various currency markets would rise or fall over the next 24 hours. No one has yet come forward to challenge the fact that the software beat them all!

The Data Logic expert system is used as an *idiot savant*: to provide split-second judgements that, taken along with the judgments of a human foreign exchange dealer, lead to what appears to be an extremely efficient way of making money. My suspicion is that there will be large transfer of expert system technology, that it will occur much later than Western governments predict, and that it will take the form that is demonstrated in the Data Logic software.

One of the interesting effects of expert system technology is that of dampening down the distorting effect of conventional software used for prediction. Nowhere is this more marked than in the financial sector described above. In September 1986 the Dow Jones index dropped by a massive hundred points for no apparent reason. There was no bad news about the dollar, the American balance of payment figures were not that bad, and there were no international crises. What seems to have happened is that a number of computers employed by stockbrokers and banks to predict share prices had all decided, at the same time, that there was to be a downward movement in share prices.

Consequently, there was a massive bout of selling. 1987 saw the biggest crash that Wall Street had ever undergone. It seems that programmed selling by computers, all acting in concert, precipitated this massive shudder in the American financial markets.

These were the first manifestations of the distorting effect of computers on the money and equity markets. Previously, there had been a number of signs that should have alerted American analysts. For example, for some time there was a distinct movement in the American markets at around 5 p.m. It used to be thought that this was due to the financial institutions winding down for the day. However, there is now considerable evidence that it was the result of computers closing down accounts.

This distortion seems to have been the fault of first-generation computer programs that use standard statistical techniques for prediction. These programs are based on the idea that if a commodity costs £3 on day 1, £6 on day 2 then, on day 3, there would be a good chance of the commodity being £9. This is a simple view of the process, but it does give an idea how predictive programs work. Normally such programs are based on extremely sophisticated probability and statistics, and involve so much number crunching that they usually require massive main-frame computers.

Prediction has now become such big business that massive starting salaries are being commanded by staff who write financial prediction programs. American 'quants' (so called because their backgrounds are in the quantitative sciences) or 'rocket scientists' are usually high-flying Ph.D.s who can earn up to $400 000 in institutions such as bond research houses or portfolio management companies. The growth in these jobs has been staggering; for example, the leading American bond-research house First Boston increased its team of bond analysts from 10 to 85 between 1981 and 1986.

The problem with first-generation programs is that essentially they use the same theory. They will all act in concert when they see the markets rising, and also when the markets fall. Consequently, as more and more companies use these programs, there is the danger of massive swings in markets, particularly in the currency markets, which are suited to technical analysis and where some degree of volatility has been the norm for the last decade. What may prevent this swing is the second generation of financial prediction programs that are based on expert system technology.

It is always difficult to predict the future in computing. However, if second-generation systems start impinging on the market then the volatility caused by the first-generation systems should decrease considerably. What would happen would be that programs that all made the same decision would be replaced by programs that mimic the human decision making that now prevails, only these decisions would be made a lot faster.

One future scenario will then be a period of increasing volatility in the money markets, with the possibility of huge swings in prices, as first-generation software starts being used more and more, followed by the dampening effect of expert system-based second-generation software. In a sense what we will have is an almost complete return to today's conditions. However, because speed is of the essence it will be those brokers and banks with the fastest programs that will win out. What is interesting about this scenario is that artificial intelligence software would not have the effect of advancing the capabilities of the companies that use the technology, but would have a potential recidivist effect.

A broker friend of mine once described the currency markets as a very sophisticated roulette game. I met him the other day, and he said nothing much had changed with the increasing use of computers for forecasting, except that the wheel was running thousands of times faster, with the ball threatening to decapitate many of the players. Let us hope for our economic health that artificial intelligence programs such as the one developed by Data Logic can slow it down.

I recently reviewed a series of artificial intelligence books that were originally published in 1980 and were reissued as paperbacks in 1986. My first reaction in starting to review them was that the publisher was attempting to make a fast buck out of the artificial intelligence boom. After all, I thought, books published as early as 1980 would have limited utility. I was very surprised by the content. Many of the sections had not dated at all; in fact, the only parts of the book that seemed out of place were those dealing with programming languages and software environments for artificial intelligence applications. Even the sections that dealt with the underlying theory of expert systems could be taught to current undergraduates. The books encapsulated, for me, all the features of artificial intelligence over the preceding two decades: the existence of a large number of extremely difficult problems such as computer vision, speech understanding, and problem-solving, with only limited progress being made in their solution; a large amount of activity and hype in one relatively small area, that of expert systems, which had resulted in spin-offs that were ripe for commercial exploitation; and a staggering increase in sophistication in the programming languages, tools, and computer hardware that could be used to develop artificial intelligence applications.[6]

Artificial intelligence workers, on the whole, seem to have done quite well in the 1980s. However, I fear that their subject has been so hyped up by interest in expert systems that any achievement short of a miracle will be regarded as abject failure.

As I was preparing this book for publication I read an announcement from the Information Engineering Directorate, the successor to the Alvey Directorate. This stated that since expert system technology had become mature, little research and development funding would be placed in this area. It seems that the worst fears of the artificial intelligence community are being realized: the last adjective I would use to describe expert system technology is 'mature'. My suspicion is that the British government, disappointed by the slow lack of progress of expert systems, has decided to drop all their involvement in the area.

# References

1.  For a well-written, but, on the whole, non-critical history of artificial intelligence see: *Machines Who Think*, P. McCorduck, San Francisco, Calif.: W. H. Freeman. 1979.

2.  Some Studies in Machine Learning Using the Game of Checkers. II. Recent Progress, A. L. Samuel, *IBM Journal of Research and Development*, **11**. 1967.

3.  On Generality and Problem Solving: A Case Study using the DENDRAL Program, E. A. Feigenbaum, B. G. Buchanan, and J. Lederberg, *Machine Intelligence 6*, New York: Elsevier. 1971.

4.  For an excellent description of some current expert systems, together with some refreshingly realistic discussions from expert system workers, see: *The AI Business, the Commercial Uses of Artificial Intelligence*, P. H. Winston and K. A. Prendergast (Eds.), Cambridge, Mass.: The MIT Press. 1985.

5.  There is now a large corpus of literature on expert systems. A good introductory text on artificial intelligence that contains excellent descriptions of expert system technology is: *Artificial Intelligence, Promise and Performance*, A. Bonnet, Englewood Cliffs, N.J.: Prentice-Hall. 1985.

6.  Some extremely sobering views about artificial intelligence, and expert systems in particular, are contained in the second part of the book: *Artificial Intelligence*, J.R. Ennals (Ed.), Maidenhead: Pergamon Infotech. 1987.

# 7

# How to develop quick and dirty software

In Chapter 1, I discussed some of the problems that occur in software development and that are due to customer requirements. Briefly, these were the poor notations used in system specifications, the size of specification documents, the technology culture-gap between the customer and the developer, the fuzziness of customer requirements, and changes external to the developer affecting these requirements during the duration of the software project.

Errors in requirements are the most serious errors that occur in a project. There is enough data from software developers that shows that an error in requirements is an order of magnitude more serious than an error in design, which, in turn, is an order of magnitude more serious than an error in programming.

In the early days, when systems were relatively simple, and when software technology was primitive, the errors that occurred were normally those that occurred during programming. For example, in 1965 the Gemini V spacecraft splashed down 100 miles from the predicted point. What had happened was that a programmer had taken a short-cut in developing a module for calculating the time elapsed since launch. This short-cut led to a slight error, which, because of the high speed of the spacecraft, was magnified into a distance error of 100 miles.

Fortunately, we are now better at testing software than we were in 1965; any developer worth his salt detects programming errors relatively quickly. However, the last twenty years have seen such a rise in the complexity of software systems, compared with advances in software technology, that it is now requirements errors that are a major problem.

One technique that has been extensively adopted by other engineering disciplines to aid development is the production of a prototype: an early version of a system that is constructed before the manufacturing process begins. In mature engineering disciplines prototypes are used for a variety of reasons. The major reason is that, because per-unit production is so costly, it is economically vital for a manufacturing company to build a few versions of a product, which are then thoroughly tested. In this way the developer can be assured that there will be a small chance of defects in a product that would lead, at best, to extensive change in the field or, at worst, mass recall of a product.

The prototyping of software products is currently a major research interest of software engineers. However, there are differences between the use made of software prototypes and of prototypes used in other industries. The per-unit production cost of software is negligible: it consists of the cost of the magnetic medium used to release the software, together with the cost of the computer time used in copying the software to this medium. Hence, software prototypes are not used for testing, but are used for requirements elicitation and clarification. Although non-software manufacturers use prototypes, or mock-ups, for a degree of requirements analysis (for example, checking that a wooden model of a product satisfies the vague non-functional requirement of 'appealing to the customer') it is true to say that their use by software developers is novel.

There are two reasons for the comparative slowness of software prototyping being adopted on software projects. First, there is the fact that it is used in a novel way as compared with the use for prototyping in other disciplines. The second reason is that, until fairly recently, the tools for producing prototypes have not been available to the software developer.

The theory behind software prototyping is simple. The developer produces a version of a software system early in a project. This normally would occur during requirements analysis. In order to produce the prototype quickly the developer usually omits or skimps the implementation of some requirements. Normally this involves forgetting about certain non-functional requirements such as response time.

The prototype is then used as a learning medium by both the developer and the customer. An initial prototype is developed and then given to the customer. This is then appraised by those staff who would normally use the finished system in its operational environment. Any discrepancies between what is delivered and what the users expect are noted; a new prototype is then developed and again evaluated. This cycle is repeated until the customer is satisfied with the system. This is then regarded as an executable version of the specification and is signed-off by the customer.

This technique views requirements analysis as a learning process that involves both the developer *and* the customer. For it to be efficient it requires close cooperation; for it to be successful it must be based on a working system. Although customers are not very good at stating what they want from a future software system, they seem to be very proficient at criticizing a current system!

There has been limited experience with prototyping so far. However, the results are extremely impressive. For example, in a large-scale experiment at the American space and defence contractor TRW, prototyped systems were developed at 40% less cost and 45% less effort than by conventional methods.[1]

There are three types of prototyping. They are throw-it-away prototyping, evolutionary prototyping, and incremental prototyping. *Throw-it-away prototyping* corresponds to the most appropriate use of the term 'prototype': the production of a quick and dirty version of a software system developed during requirements analysis that, when both customer and developer are satisfied with it, is discarded.

The need for rapid development is the greatest for throw-it-away prototyping. Since the prototype is to be used for a limited period, quality factors such as efficiency, good structure, and documentation are of little relevance. The prototype may even be implemented on hardware or within an environment other than the one required for the target system.

*Evolutionary prototyping* is in complete contrast to the throw-it-away approach; it is also in complete antithesis to current software development methods based on phases such as system design and requirements analysis. Proponents of this strategy argue that because of the nature of changing requirements software systems, once installed, evolve steadily, invalidating their original requirements. The purpose of the evolutionary prototyping approach is to introduce the system into an organization gradually, at the same time allowing it to adapt to the inevitable changes that take place within an organization as a result of using the system.

Evolutionary prototyping is by far the most powerful way of coping with change. This approach requires the system to be designed in such a way that it can cope with change *during* and *after* development. A software design technique that does not take the possibility of change into account can lead to severe problems. A typical experience of a developer is shown in this revealing extract from a description of the effect of organizational change on an existing software system[2]

> ... systems were strained badly or died as the result of corporative reorganization... An old version of a planning model was abandoned as the result of a reorganization, only to have its basic logic restructured years later... The conceptual design problem here is building systems that are truly flexible...

The major difference between evolutionary prototyping and the conventional software development scheme presented in Chapter 1, is that it is highly iterative and dynamic: each time that a system is evaluated a cycle of respecification, redesign, reimplementation, and re-evaluation takes place. This, of course, eliminates the impact of early errors during requirements analysis. Furthermore, an initial version of the system is delivered very early during a software project and, throughout development, an operational system is always available to the user. This not only supports user training alongside development but also ensures that a final system will not 'surprise' the users when eventually introduced.

The third type of prototyping is known as *incremental prototyping*. Here the system is built incrementally: one section at a time. Each time, a version of a system is delivered to the customer with more functions added. Eventually, the final system with all its functions is delivered. For example, a customer may require a system for monitoring and controlling a chemical plant. A first version might be delivered that would carry out the functions of monitoring: reading temperatures and vessel pressures, and displaying them on a variety of output hardware. The second version might deliver the functions of the first version, together with those concerned with controlling the plant: for example, shutting down chemical feeds into reactors, lowering vessel temperatures and sounding alarms at an operator's console. Finally, a third version might include all the functions of the previous versions together with facilities that enable plant operators to produce statistical data about the performance of the reactors in a plant.

This sounds similar to evolutionary prototyping. However, there is a significant difference. Incremental prototyping is based on one overall software design, established at the beginning of a software project; sections of that design are implemented gradually. With evolutionary prototyping the system does grow gradually, but in a considerably more dynamic way: a design is established at the beginning of a project, but this design can be modified considerably during a project as requirements change, and as errors in the original requirements are discovered.

The incremental approach views software development as a series of mini-projects laid end-to-end. Consequently, incremental prototyping has the major advantage which arises from small projects: that of being easy to monitor and control. However, since with incremental prototyping a design is fixed from the start of a project there is no scope for adapting to changes in requirements.

There are a large number of tools available that enable prototyped systems to be produced. They can be divided into two categories: those that prototype the functions of a system, and those that prototype the human–computer interface. The former are just concerned with demonstrating the results from a system: the latter are concerned with showing how a system will appear to the user.

One recent technique used for function prototyping is the executable specification approach. The theory behind this is that if a specification can be executed in the same way that a computer program is executed, then a prototype is available early in a project: just after requirements analysis. Unfortunately, the vast majority of requirements specifications are written in natural language, and executing such specifications, even in the next few decades, is beyond the wildest dreams of the most ardent advocates of artificial intelligence.

However, a recent trend in software engineering is the use of mathematics as a medium for specifying a system. Its use has arisen from the deficiencies in natural language that I outlined in Chapter 1 and is described in more detail in Chapters 4 and 5.

Since mathematics has a precise meaning it can theoretically be executed on a computer and a number of experimental systems have been developed that do this. These systems have a common architecture. Their major component is a translator that takes a specification expressed in mathematics and translates it into a program written in a more conventional programming language. This is then executed as any program would be.[3]

The executable specification approach has a major advantage: it does not require the developer to carry out any extra work in producing a prototype. The developer has to produce the specification as a document on which to base a design and implementation. The disadvantage with executable specification systems is that the prototypes they produce are slow; they can be very slow, in some cases. However, this matters very little: a prototype is usually discarded after the learning process between developer and customer is complete.

Another tool that can be used for function prototyping is the very high-level programming language. Normal programming languages are now extremely efficient and are tuned towards the manipulation of relatively simple objects such as numbers, names, or characters. Very high-level languages manipulate more complex objects. Two typical very high-level languages are SETL[4] and APL. SETL has extensive facilities for manipulating sets: collections of objects in which duplication is not allowed. APL is based on the manipulation of arrays: multi-dimensional collections of objects. Other very high-level languages are the artificial-intelligence languages LISP and PROLOG and the text processing language SNOBOL. The major feature of such languages is their expressibility: the fact that it is possible to write complex programs using a small amount of text. In fact it is common to write a program expressed in a very high-level language that is a tenth of the length of the equivalent program written in a conventional programming language.

Very high-level languages require rather large amounts of software support. Consequently, they can consume inordinate amounts of storage space; this makes them unsuitable for implementing a final product. They also tend to be many times slower than conventional programming languages. However, this does not diminish their utility for rapid prototyping, as time and space considerations are of little concern.

Very high-level language environments usually provide very powerful facilities for constructing and modifying programs. This enables efficient experimentation with prototypes: almost a mandatory prerequisite for effective learning by both the developer and the customer. Unfortunately, no single very high-level language is suitable for all prototyping tasks.

Another language-oriented solution to prototyping is the application-oriented high-level language. These are programming languages that contain facilities for one specific application type, for example, cost accounting or stock control. The basic idea behind application-oriented high-level languages is that if an application domain is well understood, then it is possible to provide facilities that can cater for all possible (or at least the most common) functions that would be used in that application.

Probably the best-known example of an application-oriented high-level language is MODEL.[5] This is a programming system aimed at commercial data-processing applications such as those found in banks, building societies, and wholesalers. A MODEL program simply consists of a description of data items and a set of equations that describe interrelations between the data items. This description is then processed by a translator which converts it into a program expressed in the conventional languages COBOL and PL/I. MODEL programs tend to be 5–10 times shorter than equivalent conventional programs.

By restricting themselves to small application domains, such language systems can achieve high efficiency. As a result, they have often been used to produce finished products. In addition, since they facilitate rapid development, they are able to support evolutionary prototyping. The massive productivity gains that can be achieved using such systems can be judged by the fact that in one recent experiment 13 000 lines of program code were produced for a commercial data-processing application in just six weeks.

The major advantage of application-oriented high-level languages is that they can be used by staff with little computing experience. This allows them rapidly to produce a working system that reflects their needs. The major disadvantage is their very limited scope: they are only really useful for such narrow applications as accounting, payroll, and banking, where the application area is well understood, and where there is a wealth of existing implementation history and expertise. Since the major aim of prototyping is to clarify requirements, this fact alone makes application-oriented high-level languages of limited use.

A medium for prototyping that has only recently achieved importance is the functional, or fifth-generation programming language. In Chapter 8 I describe why these languages have been developed. All that it is necessary to say, in the context of this chapter, is that they are an attempt to take full advantage of the power of the massive computer architectures that our hardware colleagues have provided for us over the last five years.

One feature of such languages, which they share with very high-level languages, is that programs for even complicated tasks occupy much less textual space than a conventional language. An example of a program in the functional programming language Miranda[6] is shown below:

```
sort [] = []
sort (a:x) = sort[b<-x | b≤a]++[a]++sort[b<-x | b>a]
```

It sorts a series of numbers in ascending order. It is not important that you understand what is happening in the program, the important point is that if I wanted to program the same problem in a conventional language it would take me at least fifteen lines of text. Since functional languages have this size advantage over conventional languages, they are capable of being used to develop systems very quickly.

Probably the most practical way of prototyping a system is via an operating system known as UNIX. An operating system is a large software system, probably the largest piece of software that runs on a computer. It controls the use of the computer by a number of programmers: it shares out memory efficiently, it ensures that each programmer receives a fair share of the power of the computer, and it administers the large store of files that users have created.

An operating system also provides sets of utility software. This is software that the designer of the operating system knows will be employed by a wide range of users. A typical utility is a sort program that takes a set of data and sorts it into ascending or descending order. Most users require a sort program; for example, commercial programmers may require it when they develop mailing list programs or directories.

The strength of UNIX is that it consists of a large number of utilities together with the mechanism to glue them together into one program. Also, the utilities can be modified by the programmer very easily to carry out different tasks. For example, a utility for selecting data from a file can be changed easily so that it picks out all the data starting with the word 'Jones'. Because of these properties UNIX can be regarded as the ultimate hacker's operating system. Many of the hackers who work in the computing industry, and there are not too many left, tend to congregate around UNIX systems. It gives them the ability to develop quick and dirty programs by selecting utilities, slightly modifying them, and then gluing them together to form one big system. The systems that are formed are usually quite inefficient. Nevertheless, they are more than adequate to demonstrate to the user as a prototype.

These, then, are the techniques that are used to demonstrate to the user what a system does, i.e. what its functions are. This is not the whole story. There is a need to demonstrate what a system looks like to a user. In many commercial data-processing applications, for example, airline reservation systems, hotel booking systems, and foreign exchange dealing systems, a large number of vdu screens are used to communicate with the user. For such applications the customer is intensely interested in how the system looks to its users, i.e. what the human–computer interface looks like.

There are a very limited number of techniques that can be used to carry out prototyping of the human–computer interface. Work in the area lags well behind that on prototyping the functions of a system. One promising technique involves the use of a formal grammar. This is a mathematical notation that is used to define programming languages. If you look at the back of any programming language manual you will find, as an appendix, a formal grammar that defines the language unambiguously. An example of a formal grammar, used in defining a simple interface to a foreign-exchange dealing system, is shown below. The system allows a dealer to find out the value of one of three currencies (Yen, Dollar, Pound) on a particular date and time.

```
<command>::=(<Yen_command>|<Dollar_command>|<Pound_command>)
                <date_ and_time>
<Yen_command> ::= YEN
<Dollar_command> ::= DOLLAR
<Pound_command> ::= POUND
```

```
<date_and_time> ::= <day> <month> <time>
<day> ::= <integer>
<month> ::= JAN I FEB I MAR I APR I MAY I JUN I JUL I AUG I SEP I
            OCTINOV I DEC
<time> ::= <integer> : <integer>
```

This looks pretty daunting, but once you are use to reading formal grammars it becomes a trivial task to understand them. The first and second lines state that a command typed in by a foreign exchange dealer will either be a Yen command, a Dollar command, or a Pound command, the I character that separates them stands for 'or'. When a word is enclosed in the brackets <> it means that that word is defined further in the formal grammar description. The first line also states that after the user has typed in either a Yen command, a Dollar command, or a Pound command, he types in a date, this is the date for which he requires currency information.

The Yen command is defined on the third line; all it entails is the user typing in the characters YEN. The Dollar and Pound commands are similar to this. The sixth line defines what is meant by a date and time. It states that a date and time consists of a day, followed by a month and terminated by a time. The seventh line defines a day to be an integer. The eighth and ninth lines define a month to be either the characters JAN, or the characters FEB, etc.

Finally, the tenth line defines a time to be an integer, followed by a colon and then terminated by an integer. The first integer is the hour and the second integer is the minute. Thus, a valid date and time typed in by the user would be 21 JAN 12:30. What has been omitted is a definition of an integer; however, this definition is similar to the rest shown above. The full definition shown above describes a command such as DOLLAR 23 FEB 14:30. This would display the value of the dollar at 14:30 on the 23rd of February.

A number of systems have been developed that take such a description of an interface and produce it directly on a screen.[7] These systems usually process a more complicated notation than the one shown above, which is a little too simple to be useful; for example, it doesn't allow any facilities for discovering errors such as a user typing in an invalid date such as 45 SEP.

Another technique used for prototyping uses a graphic notation involving *state transition diagrams*. Such diagrams describes the input, output, and transitions that occur during interaction with the computer. An example is shown in Figure 7.1. It shows the interface between a computer operator and the software that controls a network of computers. The computer operator often wants to find out who is currently using the network, how busy a particular computer processor is, and how much memory is being used by an particular computer.

To enable him to do this three commands are provided they are: 'memory load', 'users', and 'processor load'. All the operator has to do is to type in the command corresponding to the query he has to make. The 'processor load' and 'memory load' commands also require the operator to type in the name of the computer whose resource utilization is being queried.

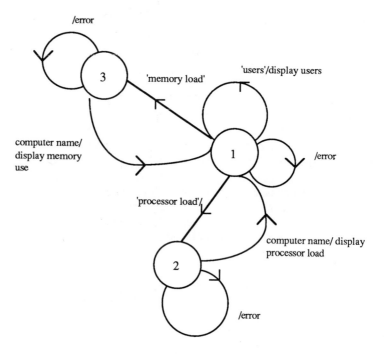

**Figure 7.1.** A state transition diagram.

The state transition diagram consist of circles known as states. When an interface is within one of these states it is waiting for something to happen. The diagram above shows three states. State 1 is when the interface is waiting for the operator to type in a command. When a command is typed in the interface moves to another state, and an action is taken. Each state consist of a number of lines leading from it to other states. Each line is labelled with two sets of words separated by the / character. The first set of words represents the input that has to occur if the line is to be traversed, the second set of words represents the action that is taken when the traversal occurs.

The decision about which line is taken depends on what has been typed in. For example, in the diagram above, state 1 has four lines emanating from it. If the operator types in the command 'processor load' then the line that leads to state 2 is taken; since the set of words following the / is empty no action is taken. The interface is now in state 2. In this state it is waiting for the name of the computer that the operator is to type in. If a valid computer name is typed in then the line leading to state 1 is traversed, and the set of words following the /

on the line tells us that the processor load on that computer is displayed. If the operator types a computer name that the interface does not recognize, perhaps because he mis-typed a character, then the other line leading from state 2 is taken. This returns the interface to state 2, and displays the fact that an error has occurred. The interface is again awaiting a correct computer name.

In this way the state transition diagram represents the states that an interface goes through during its interaction with a human operator. A number of programs have been built that process a state diagram description of an interface and automatically synthesize a prototype interface.[8]

Another technique involves the use of a descriptive language that defines an interface. The user of such a system types in a succinct description of an interface. This is processed by a specialized program and the interface is displayed. Each time that a screen is displayed it is stored in a central database and can be retrieved easily.[9]

Probably one of the most obvious ways for providing prototyping tools for the human–computer interface is to build facilities into a programming language that provide the programmer with the ability to describe dialogues, sketch out what screens should look like, and describe how the user should respond. Unhappily, language designers have until fairly recently, almost to a person, ignored this aspect of programming language design. The majority of programming languages in use today, including modern fifth-generation languages could have had their human–computer facilities designed in the early 1960s. The designers of such languages tend to be more concerned with the elegance of the structures used for the processing rather than worrying about how to communicate with the user.

One of the heartening characteristics of prototyping today is the wide availability of tools. Prototyping corresponds to the intuitively appealing idea that experiencing is vastly superior to reading. However, there is a problem, and it is quite a large one: the current phase-oriented method that I described in Chapter 1 falls short of what is required for a prototyping project. Prototyping is a much more dynamic process than conventional software development: it involves a seemingly endless cycle of build, evaluate, modify, re-evaluate; few managers are used to this degree of dynamic in a project, and it is hardly surprising that when prototyping projects undergo squalls and, in some cases, hurricanes, it is management, rather than tools and techniques, that seem at fault.

There are a number of simple guidelines that would help any manager control a software project. The first guideline is based on the recognition that there are three sorts of prototyping: throw-it-away prototyping, evolutionary prototyping, and incremental prototyping. The first decision that a project manager has to make about prototyping is which of these models to adopt. This decision depends on the volatility of the application area. If an application is novel, will take a number of years to complete, and is also in an area where change is common during the duration of a project, for example in a defence application, then evolutionary prototyping would seem the natural choice. A typical application that would benefit from evolutionary prototyping is an air defence system. Such a system is particularly sensitive to rapid changes in both attack and defence technology.

If the application was one where, once customer requirements are established, they change very little, or where project duration is short, then throw-it-away prototyping would be the choice. A typical application where this form of prototyping would be used is an order-processing system for a wholesaler.

If the application was one where the functions of a proposed system could be partitioned into sets of mutually exclusive groups that are not related to each other, and where there is not much requirements volatility, then incremental prototyping would be a good choice. A typical application would be a commercial data-processing system that processed unrelated queries on a central database from a wide variety of users such as managers, stock-clerks, and accountants.

It is probably worth giving one word of warning at this stage. Both incremental and throw-it-away prototyping fit reasonably well into conventional project frameworks. Incremental prototyping just consists of a series of conventional mini-projects, while throw-it-away prototyping involves a cycle of prototype evaluations, followed by conventional software project activities.

Evolutionary prototyping is a rather different proposition. It involves a dynamic approach to development throughout a project. If you have very little expertise in prototyping, then do not attempt evolutionary prototyping. Allow your staff to cut their teeth on incremental and throw-it-away prototyping before they attempt the more difficult task.

The next question the manager has to ask is what parts of a system need to be prototyped: the functional part or the human–computer interface. It can be a major effort to prototype both, so he has to examine the nature of the system to be developed: if the system contains a lot of user interaction, then concentrate on the user interface; if functionality dominates, say in an air defence system, then prototype the functions. This advice may seem platitudinous. However, it is clear from looking at a number of prototyping failures that little consideration of the prototyping area and the prototyping options took place.

Once the model of prototyping has been decided on, the next step is for the manager to decide on the prototyping objectives. This involves looking at what parts of the system, or the developmental process, are going to be ignored or compromised. A prototype has to be deficient with respect to the final system that it represents: it it wasn't then it would be the system. The developer has to decide what needs to be compromised in order to deliver a prototype quickly. Typically, he may decide to ignore non-functional characteristics such as response time, memory size, or maintainability; or again, he may decide to implement a subset of the system's functions; or he may decide to ignore the stringent and time-consuming quality assurance standards adopted by his company.

The prototyping objectives, the prototyping model adopted, a description of how prototyping is to be achieved, and the use that is to be made of the prototype, should all be written into a document known as the prototyping plan. It should form an important part of the project plan, and should be delivered in a detailed form with a preliminary draft of the project plan. The prototyping plan should be itemized as a separate deliverable, and should be signed-off by the customer before the first prototyping activities commence.

The signing-off process is vital. A number of prototyping projects have failed — and failed disastrously — when the customer has evaluated a prototype, declared himself pleased, and promptly demanded the prototype for production use. The customer's pleasure at receiving a software system that, at last, meets his needs, soon disappears when he realizes that the system runs as fast as syrup in a production environment, or contains errors due to the developer's relaxing his quality assurance standards. Don't feel that you should resist a demand from a customer for the use of a prototype: there are some excellent uses of prototypes over and above requirements clarification, for example, they can be used for early staff training and, after all, the customer as paymaster has every right to ask for the prototype. However, what should be made very clear in the prototyping plan are the assumptions the developer is making about customer use of the prototype.

A tool that is becoming a prerequisite for any prototyping project is an automated configuration management system. Such a system stores versions of a system together with its associated documents. It allows the developer to return to the state a project in the past and retrieve previous versions of a software system. In a prototyping project there will be a need to store the program code of each prototype, together with the evaluation forms that record the customers reaction to that version, and the minutes of any evaluation meeting which considered that version.

Prototyping teams have often been faced with a customer who has suddenly stated ' You know this prototype isn't much of an improvement over the one we examined two Thursdays ago. Come to think of it, that prototype was much better!' With an automated configuration management system, the prototyping team can play back the project to any arbitrary moment in time extremely easily. Without an automated configuration management system, dealing with such requests can be extremely tedious. In fact, for an evolutionary prototyping project such a system is virtually mandatory.

Another major concern for the project manager is the selection of prototyping staff. There are a number of sensible principles. First, keep the prototyping team as small as possible. Prototyping is a communication-intensive approach and a smaller team facilitates this, cuts down on documentation, and enables faster iteration between prototype versions. In staffing the project you should always pick staff who have an open attitude to criticism. Many designers tend to be ego-centred, and regard their systems as just being extensions of themselves. Introducing such staff on a prototyping project, where minute, critical judgement is the order of the day, can lead to extremely ineffective results. In choosing staff for the prototyping project always pick staff with good social skills, even if you may be worried about their technical skills. Prototyping is a systems analysis technique, and the communication skills important for the analyst should be sought for in staff selected to carry out prototyping.

Staffing is also important from the customer side. The developer has to ensure that sufficient time has been allocated by the customer to enable his staff to take part in the evaluation sessions, and that the same staff are used from session to session. It is important to stress to the customer that, except for the most important of reasons, no substitution should be allowed. This point is so important it should be written into the project plan and agreed by the customer.

One of the activities that has been flagged by commentators as being potentially the most troublesome is the prototype evaluation process. They have argued that because of the dynamic nature of this process, there is always the temptation by the customer to think of some more new requirements and to ask for yet another prototype. This has rarely happened. There are good economic reasons for this: the customer perceives that, at a certain point, any more evaluation and prototype building would start putting the delivery time of the system into jeopardy. This tends to concentrate his mind.

Consequently, it is a good idea for the project manager to flag a time in his project plan when the evaluation process has to end. Don't forget too that the prototyping process should be followed by a process of system specification when staff deconstruct the software prototype and write down what it does. Don't underestimate the time to do this. It's certainly much shorter than the specification time on a normal project but it can occupy a fair amount of project resource.

Much of the advice in the last half of this chapter might just seem common sense. However, I have seen projects wallow, and even fail, through not following at least one of the points I make above. If there is one guiding principle that has emerged from the history of prototyping it is this: just because the prototyping process seems haphazard and meandering don't imagine haphazard and meandering management techniques can be used, the reverse is true!

# References

1.  Prototyping versus Specifying: a Multiproject Experience, B. W. Boehm, T. E. Gray, and T. Seewaldt, *IEEE Transactions on Software Engineering*, **10**, 3. 1984.

2.  *Decision Support Systems — Current Practice and Continuing Challenges*, S.A. Alter, Reading, Mass.: Addison-Wesley. 1980.

3.  One of the best known systems for software prototyping is described in the paper: Functional Programming, Formal Specification and Rapid Prototyping, P. Henderson, *IEEE Transactions on Software Engineering*, **12**, 2. 1986.

4.  *Programming With Sets: An Introduction to SETL*, J. T. Schwartz *et al.*, New York: Springer Verlag. 1986.

5.  Compilation of Non-procedural Specifications into Computer Programs, N. S. Prywes and A. A. Pnueli, *IEEE Transactions on Software Engineering*, **9**, 3. 1983.

6.  A good introduction to Miranda can be found in David Turner's paper: Functional Programs as Executable Specifications. in *Mathematical Logic and Programming Languages*, C. A. R. Hoare and J. Sheperdson (Eds.), Englewood Cliffs, N.J: Prentice-Hall.1985.

7.  One example is described in the paper: Prototyping and Simulation Tools for User/computer Dialogue Design, P. R. Hanau and D. R. Lenorovitz, *Computer Graphics*, **14**, 2. 1980.

8.  Probably the best such system was developed by the American Computer Scientist, Tony Wasserman. It is described in the paper: Extending State Transition Diagrams for the Specification of Human Computer Interaction, A. D. Wasserman, *IEEE Transactions on Software Engineering*, **11**, 8. 1985.

9.  One typical system is described in: HIBOL, A Language for Fast Prototyping in Data Processing Environments, A. Mittermeir, *ACM SIGSOFT Software Engineering Notes*, **7**, 5. 1982.

# 8

# Just like a magic machine

Wouldn't it be nice to write a specification for a computer program, type it into your computer and, after not too long a wait, have it produce the program that corresponds to the specification. It sounds rather like science fiction. However, it is the serious aim of a number of research groups scattered throughout the world.

To develop such an automatic programming system requires a number of components. The major one is a new type of programming language that can be manipulated inside an automatic programming system. To examine the state of automatic programming it is worth looking at some computing history and returning to 1977.

Each year the prestigious American Association for Computing Machinery gives its Turing award to a scientist who has made major contributions to computer science. The award is normally given at the Association's annual conference, and the occasion is normally accompanied by a rosy glow of congratulation and an uncontroversial acceptance speech. However, the 1977 award ceremony was rather different from this.

The recipient was John Backus of IBM's San Jose Research Laboratory. Backus was the father of the FORTRAN programming language and played an important part in the definition of modern programming languages. It was Backus, more than any other computer scientist, who freed generations of programmers from the tedium of writing assembler programs. His work led to the emergence of more and more powerful high-level languages such as ALGOL, Pascal, and Ada. His research also enabled computer scientists easily to produce compilers: programs that translated high-level languages into the language of the computer.

In his acceptance speech[1] Backus repudiated all his previous work and advocated the use of a new generation of functional programming languages. It was almost as if the Pope had declared that he had decided to become a Methodist! A silent audience, many of whom had never even heard of functional languages, listened as Backus explained how he had come to the conclusion that conventional programming languages had served their purpose, but had now become obsolete, and that a radical approach to programming was required.

What had motivated Backus was the problems he could see occurring in the future with computer hardware. All computers from the first primitive relay-based machines up to current sophisticated 32-bit micros have employed the same architecture. It is known as the Von-Neumann architecture, after John von Neumann who first postulated the idea that a machine could store programming instructions and act upon them. A Von-Neumann computer consists of input/output devices, backing storage for long term data, main storage, and a processor. The operation of the Von-Neumann computer relies on programs stored in main storage. It consists of the processor retrieving programming instructions one at a time and executing them. This leads to a bottleneck in a computer system whereby instructions, which can only be transferred one at a time, are waiting for execution. Moreover, even machines with a few processors require very painstaking and error-prone programming to squeeze the full power from them.

The first attempts at eliminating this bottleneck involved hardware manufacturers constructing computers with a small number of processors. Although this solution initially reduced the backlog and, consequently, produced faster computers it was found that just adding processors *ad infinitum* actually lead to a degradation in performance.

The reason for this is straightforward. In order to carry out a task with a number of processors, the conventional Von-Neumann computer has to allow its processors to communicate and synchronize with each other. The larger the number of processors the larger the amount of synchronization required. In fact, the amount of synchronization rises almost exponentially. Thus, when computer scientists connected more than about four processor together they discovered that the processors were almost totally involved in passing messages to each other rather than doing useful work. There thus seems to be an upper limit to the power of the Von-Neumann computer, an upper limit that not even massive increases in speed due to advances in silicon technology could surpass.

A second development that persuaded Backus to recant was the explosive growth of programming languages, a growth that was in the wrong direction. It is certainly true that we have come along way since the late 1940s. The early computers were programmed by throwing switches that represented binary patterns that corresponded to programming instructions. We now use powerful high-level languages that have almost completely eliminated this drudgery. However, the growth of high-level languages has also brought with it worries. Programming productivity has lagged well behind the complexity of the systems that developers are now called upon to build.

This has lead to programming languages that are getting bigger and more complicated. The prime example of this is Ada, the recent language adopted by the American Department of Defense, which dwarfs the early programming languages FORTRAN and COBOL.[2] It has seemed to a number of researchers that computer scientists have devised programming languages that are even more complicated than the tasks which they are called upon to perform. Moreover, it has resulted in programming languages that are mathematically intractable.

One of the major aims of computer science is devise programming languages whose programs can be reasoned about mathematically. Such languages should enable us to write a specification of a system in mathematics, construct the programs that make up the system and, by informal and formal mathematical reasoning demonstrate that the program meets its specification.

Certainly, if software engineering is to mirror other engineering disciplines, for example, civil engineering or electrical engineering, then the use of mathematics as a medium for specification and the verification of programs should be a major aim of language designers. Unfortunately, each new language that has been devised has been more mathematically complex than the previous one. Scientists thought a language like Pascal was poor in this respect. However, compared to Ada it is a masterpiece of mathematical elegance!

Backus' speech was a call for minimalism in programming language design. He pointed out the that baroque growth of programming languages had lead to the creation of software monsters and that the Von-Neumann architecture was a very poor base for multi-processor systems. He proposed that only a completely new language type: the functional language, could release us from present constrictions.

Such languages are based on recursion equations. An example of a set of recursion equations is shown below. It is taken from a functional programming language called HOPE[3] that has been developed at Imperial College, London.

```
average(l) <= sum(l) div count(l)
sum(nil) <= 0
sum(n::l) <= n+sum(l)
count(nil) <=0
count(n::l) <= 1+count(l)
```

The first line is straightforward. It states that the average of a list of numbers $l$ is equal to the sum of the numbers in $l$ divided by the count of the numbers in $l$. The symbols <= stand for the words: 'is equal to'. The next two lines defines *sum*. The second line states that the sum of the empty list of numbers (nil) is zero. The third line states that the sum of a list containing a number $n$ followed by a list $l$ is equal to $n$ plus the sum of the numbers in $l$. The fourth and fifth lines define what is meant by *count*. The fourth line states that the count of the number of elements in an empty list (nil) is zero. The fifth line states that the count of the elements in a list consisting of a number $n$ followed by a list $l$ of numbers is equal to 1 plus the count of the elements in $l$.

Notice how different this program is compared with a typical Von-Neumann program that might be written in a language such as COBOL. Such a program would have a loop and would mimic the action of the computer in retrieving data, counting it, and adding it to a partial sum. Each instruction in the language would have to wait to travel down the bottleneck from main store to the processor to be executed. The functional program consists of a series of equations, parts of which can be shared between large numbers of processors, with very little communicational overhead. Moreover, it is possible to reason mathematically with such languages, in the same way that a bridge designer explores a specification for a bridge in order to check on its safety.

As well as their simplicity and their use on multi-processor computing systems, functional languages also have a vitally important property that is of interest to scientists engaged in research in automatic programming. Such scientists have, over the past twenty years, been attempting to automate the process of software construction, and produce development systems in which a specification can be fed in at one end and a correct program emerges at the other.

Currently we develop software by first writing a specification. Usually this specification is written in English. This is then transformed into a design that represents the architecture of a system. The design, which is normally expressed in a graphic notation, is transformed into a program written in a programming language.

There are major disadvantages in this. First, as I have stated earlier in this book, English is not a good medium for expressing the functionality of a software system. It is ideal as a medium for poems and novels but it lacks precision. Graphic notations are also fuzzy in this respect. This lack of precision early on in a software project usually creates errors that reverberate throughout the project, and can cause massive over-spends. Errors also occur at the boundary of specification and design and also at the boundary of design and programming owing to changes in notation.

A second disadvantage is that attempting to get a customer to understand just exactly what he is going to receive as a software system from a reading of specification documents is, for complex systems, almost impossible. Project managers have whole portfolios of stories of occasions when an inordinate amount of time was spent validating a specification with a customer, checking for correctness, lack of ambiguity, and completeness, only for the customer to announce at the end of the project that the delivered software did not meet his requirements.

How then does functional programming promise to alleviate these problems? The key to the solution arises from a research area known as transformational programming. For a number of years computer scientists have been attempting to devise techniques whereby a specification could be automatically transformed into a program. All a software developer would need to do is write the specification and a separate computer program would produce the finished system. Unfortunately, the research that was carried out prior to the advent of functional languages has been spectacularly unsuccessful. However, one of the properties of functional languages is that it is possible to construct functional programs that look like a mathematical specification of what a system is intended to do. Unfortunately, these programs tend to be inefficient. However, because functional languages are a mathematical notation, programs expressed in that notation can be manipulated just like equations and turned into more efficient programs.

The last few years have seen research results emerge that indicate that, by a process of transformation, this initial inefficient program can be changed into successively more efficient functional programs. These transformations are conceptually similar to what the old-time computer scientists knew as code optimization. The very early programming-language compilers produced very inefficient machine programs; these had to be optimized by another program in order for the computer to be used efficiently. The transformations on functional programs differ from this only in that they operate at a much higher level. Currently transformations are normally carried out by hand. However, there is an increasing amount of research aimed at automating this process.

This approach to program construction would eliminate many of the problems due to differing software notations: the only notation that the developer would need to know is that subset of the functional language used for specification.

The use of functional languages also overcomes the problem of the customer being unable to comprehend the nature of a software system early in a project. Since a specification written using a functional programming language is executable, then a version of the software system is available early on in the project. This version will be very inefficient and, consequently, will never be used as a production program. However, it is efficient enough to be used to give the customer an idea of what his software system will look like. Thus, it acts as a prototype that can be discussed, tried out in the customer's work environment and, finally, signed off as a correct reflection of the customer's needs. This can then be used as a standard against which subsequent, more efficient versions of the software can be compared.

No longer would customer and developer wrangle over volumes of natural-language specification. If there is a dispute over the function of a delivered software system then all that is needed to resolve it is for the prototype and the delivered system to be checked out against live data The results can be examined with a simple file comparator. If they agree, the customer is at fault: the delivered software meets its specification. If they do not agree, the developer is at fault: the software has deviated from the specification.

The United Kingdom is the world leader in the design and implementation of functional languages. The probable reason for this is that this country has had a tradition of mathematics-based computer science research. Unfortunately, until fairly recently the research work was centred on a small number of universities. However, the recent British government's Alvey Programme has as one of it main aims the production of computer architectures capable of supporting functional languages.

In conjunction with this the Alvey software engineering programme aims to produce third generation integrated program support environments (IPSEs). An IPSE is a set of software tools configured around a central database of project data such as version numbers, change requests, and documentation.

IPSEs are distinguished by the nature of the database. A first-generation IPSE is configured around conventional files. Second-generation IPSEs would be configured around a database system. These are still a relatively long term prospect. Finally, third-generation IPSEs would be configured around a knowledge base, would support functional programming and would rely on artificial intelligence technology. This technology would be used to guide the transformation process that can be applied to functional programming languages. A typical architecture for the functional programming kernel of a third-generation IPSE is shown in Figure 8.1.

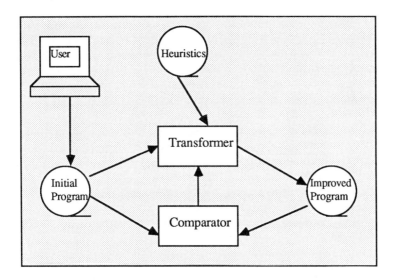

**Figure 8.1.** Architecture of the kernel of a third-generation IPSE.

The heart of the kernel is a transformer, this takes the initial version of the program and applies a set of transformational rules to produce a more efficient program. These rules are embodied in a stored set of heuristics that have been culled from experts in program transformation. When a more efficient program has been produced it is executed, and its time is compared with that of the original program by means of a comparator; if it exceeds the run time of this program by a specified amount then it is presented to the user. If not the system uses some more heuristics to improve the original program. The process terminates when the performance of the transformed program exceeds a limit specified by the user.

This, then, is the good news. The bad news is that there are still major difficulties in reaching the final goal of an automatic programming system. First, to be usable, functional languages need new hardware architectures. The majority of functional languages that have been implemented have used Von-Neumann architectures. The resulting execution speeds have been very slow indeed. There are a number of new architecture projects currently in existence, and only when one of them delivers the goods will functional programming become viable. This is quite a novelty. For the first time for thirty years the software developers are waiting on the hardware developers! Unfortunately, for once the progress of hardware colleagues has been quite slow.

The second factor is that much more experience is needed of functional programming in industrial environments. In the main, most of the experience gained in the use of these languages has been in the universities on toy problems. Although it is now clear that functional programming can be used in applications areas such as system software and commercial data processing, it is still not clear whether they are viable for areas such as real-time processing

The third factor is education and training. Functional programming languages hold out the hope of a massive reduction in the amount of programming that will be carried out in the future. Unfortunately, the level of mathematical skills required to carry out functional programming is very high. Indeed, the type of mathematics required is very rarely taught in our schools and colleges in sufficient depth.

The British education system still teaches the mathematics required for the pure sciences and engineering. This mathematics has real numbers as its base. The mathematics required for functional programming is based on a branch of mathematics known as discrete mathematics. It includes set theory and formal logic and is more concerned with discrete objects. Such mathematics still takes a very poor second place in many syllabuses.

Moreover, functional programming requires a different way of thinking about a software problem. Currently, we design programs by thinking of them in terms of a series of steps. For example, searching a table can be thought of as looking at an entry, examining that entry, stopping if it was the required entry, and moving to the next entry if it wasn't. However, functional programming requires a much more static mathematical approach to problem solving; an approach that we are not used to in everyday life and one that is rarely taught. If functional programming is to become a force in computing over the next years, it may be that the most urgent issue that will have to be addressed will be that of training and education.

However, the major problem in developing automatic programming systems is the actual manipulations of the initial, inefficient program that are required to produce a production program. Whenever I read a paper describing how an initial specification was transformed into a final functional program[4] I come away with a sense of awe and frustration. The sense of awe comes from my having had a small peep at one of the great problems of computer science (if the Nobel prize is ever given to a software researcher, the solution to the problem of automatic programming would surely be an excellent reason for the award). My sense of frustration comes from an increasing conviction that so many higher-order cognitive processes are involved that we may never automate it. I once attended a conference on functional programming in America. At one of the sessions an American computer scientist described the process whereby a specification would be transformed into a working program. He described the system as 'just like a magic machine'. When I was very young I used to have such a machine. You would feed a blank sheet of paper in at one end and out would come a pound note. The trick, of course, was to load the pound note in before you used the magic machine and, by dint of a clever roller mechanism, it would produce the note. Transformational programming systems remind me of such machines, although, if pressed, I would have to admit that, currently, in order to get your pound note, you need only load 95p into the machine.

Nevertheless, even if we never solve the problem of automatic programming there will be valuable spin-offs. Functional languages are very impressive. Compared to the programming languages we use today they are much more elegant, less obscure, and are capable of producing software very quickly.

## References

1. This speech is reproduced in full in: Can Programming be Liberated from the Von Neumann Style? A Functional Style and its Algebra of Programs, *Communications of the ACM*, **21**, 7. 1978.

2. A good example of a polemic against complication in programming languages, and in Ada in particular, is contained in Tony Hoare's paper: The Emperor's New Clothes, C. A. R Hoare, *Communications of the ACM*, **24**, 2. 1981.

3. A good introduction to HOPE, together with other accounts of Imperial College work on functional languages, is in a collection of papers edited by Sue Eisenbach: *Functional Programming: Languages, Tools and Architectures*, S. Eisenbach (Ed.), Chichester, U.K.: Ellis Horwood. 1987.

4. For example, John Darlington's paper: The Structured Derivation of Algorithm Derivations, J. Darlington, in *Algorithmic Languages*, J. W. De Bakker and J.C. Van Vliet (Eds.), Amsterdam: North Holland. 1981.

# 9

# Software that learns

One of the bottlenecks in the development of an expert system is that of discovering the rules that an expert uses. The process of knowledge elicitation is so painful that artificial intelligence workers now refer to a phenomenon known as the 'knowledge bottleneck'. This is a term used to describe the fact that we have now reached the stage in expert system technology where there are a large number of software systems, programming languages, and microcomputers that are aimed at developing expert systems, but there is a log-jam in interviewing human experts and extracting the rules they use.

One solution that has been put forward to solve this problem is to dispense with the human expert, and just rely on a large corpus of existing examples of the problem to be solved, together with their corresponding results. This would involve building a software system that learns from particular instances of a problem. For example, a learning program for diagnosing blood disease might be presented with a set of symptoms from a patient (white cell count, red cell count, blood pressure, etc) together with the diagnosis of a human expert. After processing a large number of symptoms and diagnoses, such a program would be able to spot trends in the data and, when given a fresh set of symptoms, would be able to produce a diagnosis.

Such a learning program might operate in the same way that a human expert would work: classifying the data presented to it, attempting to verify hypotheses about values of the data affecting the diagnosis, discarding unimportant factors, and, finally, coming up with rules that relate the factors to the diagnosis. As a rather simple example of such reasoning consider Table 9.1.

**Table 9.1**

| A | B | C | R |
|---|---|---|---|
| 5 | 1 | 1 | 26.00 |
| 10 | 2 | 2 | 100.50 |
| 15 | 4 | 3 | 225.33 |
| 20 | 8 | 4 | 400.25 |

Assume that $A$, $B$, and $C$ are factors such as a patient's blood pressure, heart rate, etc., while $R$ is a result that a human expert infers from the factors, say the number of milligrams of a chemical to be injected into the patient over a period of time. A learning program would examine each set of factors and start to make inferences about how they affect the value of the result. The first thing that would be noticed by such a program would be that the result rose very quickly. This would suggest that it varied as a power of one of the factors. The system then might try a number of values of a power; it might try $A^2$, $A^3$, $A^4$ etc. and then $B^2$, $B^3$, $B^4$ and so on, checking for a fit. It would soon discover that the factor $A$, when squared, seemed to give the best fit. The next stage would be to look at how other factors might affect the result. The program would soon discover that when $1/C$ was added to $A^2$ the result was matched, and that, furthermore, factor $B$ was irrelevant to the process of inferring the result. Thus, when presented with a further set of data the program would be able to predict a result.

Now the discussion above was highly artificial. First, no self-respecting user of a learning program would employ it after it had been set loose on only three data sets. Second, the technique that I described was primitive and would not be found in any contemporary learning programs. Third, very rarely do you get an exact fit between factors and a result. Fourth, the application was very unrealistic. Nevertheless, it gives an idea of the process of formulating rules based on sets of data that represent factors together with the equivalent result.

The description above is of only one technique for computer learning, based on learning by example; other techniques have also been used. The simplest is rote learning, whereby a program is given a set of factor values and a result. Whenever the user of such a learning program questions it, using a set of facts, it looks up these facts in its store, and if they match with a set that it has already been taught, it extracts the corresponding result.

A second technique is based on learning by analogy, here a learning program discovers a similar situation that it has encountered before. For example, a learning program might be employed to navigate around a floor. Previously, it discovered that when it steered towards a large oblong object it was prevented from moving forward; it would use learning by analogy to prevent it from steering towards large square objects.

The final technique, and the most demanding in terms of software development, is learning by observation and discovery. A learning program based on this idea would examine its own knowledge in an attempt to find regularities and similar rules from which it could devise new laws and facts. In the remainder of this chapter, two examples of learning programs are described. One is based on learning by example; the other on learning by observation and discovery. They have been purposely selected to illustrate one trend in artificial intelligence research.

The technique that, virtually overnight, brought home the practicality of machine learning to computer scientists was devised by an Australian

researcher, Ross Quinlan,[1] and is the classical example of learning by example.
His technique is based on classifying data using a structure known as a
*classification tree*. In describing the technique I shall use an example found in a
very readable introduction to Quinlan's work[2] It concerns an investment strategy
for backing information technology companies. There are a number of factors
that a financial analyst needs to look at when deciding on the risk inherent in
sinking money into an information technology company. The first question that
is often asked is what is the nature of the company: hardware or software?
Another question is whether the company's main product is new, in the middle
of its life, or old. A third question is whether there is significant existing
competition for the company's product.

Assume that Table 9.2 below contains values of these factors, for a number
of companies, together with the result which describes the profit movement of
the company.

**Table 9.2**

| Profit | Age | Competition | Type |
|--------|---------|-------------|----------|
| Down | Old | No | Software |
| Down | Midlife | Yes | Software |
| Up | Midlife | No | Hardware |
| Down | Old | No | Hardware |
| Up | New | No | Hardware |
| Up | New | No | Software |
| Up | Midlife | No | Software |
| Up | New | Yes | Software |
| Down | Midlife | Yes | Hardware |
| Down | Old | Yes | Software |

The first entry states that this company is a software company with no
competition, with a product that is towards the end of its life and whose profits
were down last year. The third entry shows a hardware company that has no
competition, markets a product that is in the middle of its life, and whose profits
were up last year.

Quinlan's method involved building a structure known as a classification tree.
Such a tree shows the division of the data shown in the table above into
categories. The first stage in building the tree is to select a factor and divide the
set of data above into sets corresponding to each factor. This is shown below in
Figure 9.1 for the factor age.

**Figure 9.1**. Classification tree.

The structure in Figure 9.1 is the classification tree. Whenever a program based on Quinlan's technique is used, this tree is stored in main memory of the computer. The factor chosen to construct the decision tree above was the age of the product. The tree shows that if the product was old then the profits were down, and if the product was new then the profits were up. It is still problematic what happens if the product is in the middle of its life. In order to cater for this the next stage of Quinlan's technique is to split up the data for the midlife products (Figure 9.2.).

All the users of a program based on Quinlan's technique has to do, is to follow the arrows across, making a decision whenever a factor is encountered. For example, assume that I wanted to find out the investment possibilities of a company that has a midlife software product with no competition. The first decision concerns the age of the product; this takes the program down the lowest branch of the diagram. Then the next decision concerns the competition for the product. Since there is no competition the program moves to the uppermost branch of this decision and discovers, irrespective of whether the product is software or hardware, a profit can be expected.

The decision about the order in which factors are chosen to carry out the classification is critical. Rather than selecting on age, another factor could have been selected. Quinlan's technique uses a branch of mathematics known as information theory to select the optimum ordering of factors.

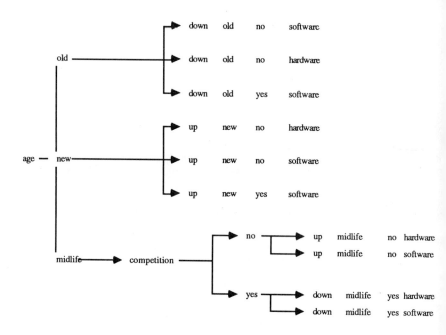

**Figure 9.2.**

A deeper use of learning programs is being explored at Carnegie Mellon University in the United States. Nobel-prize-winning researcher Herb Simon is trying to develop programs that attempt to discover scientific laws from experimental data. In the late 1970s Simon had become concerned with what he saw as an unhealthy preoccupation in the philosophy of science with verificationism: the process of postulating a scientific theory and then checking it by techniques that involve observing real-world events. The emphasis is on a theory being discovered by some flash of inspiration and the purpose of experiments is to attempt to demolish a theory. This spirit, which still runs through the philosophy of science, was a product of two massively influential philosophers of science, Thomas Kuhn and Karl Popper, who both, directly or indirectly, denied the systematic use of rules, procedures, and heuristics by scientists in deriving theories after observation of real-life events.

Simon's research echoed the work of Francis Bacon in the seventeenth century and that of John Stuart Mill in the nineteenth century. Both were concerned with deriving advice and heuristics for effecting the process of scientific discovery. The major aim of Simon's work is to develop what he calls a normative theory of scientific discovery. This does not mean that such a theory encompass a set of rules for conclusively discovering a scientific law; it is more a set of criteria for judging the efficacy and efficiency of the processes used to discover scientific theories.

To test out his theories, Simon and his co-workers developed a series of computer programs that examined data from classical experiments, and attempted to infer the laws that lay behind the data. The programs were named *Bacon.1* to *Bacon.5*, after Francis Bacon, whom Simon regarded as a major influence on his work on scientific discovery. In order to give you a flavour of how one of the programs worked (Bacon.1), a sample from a session with Bacon.1 is shown below. The heuristics that Bacon.1 uses to discover scientific laws are relatively simple; they are:

If the values of a term are constant, then infer that the term always has that value.

If the values of two numerical terms increase together then consider their ratio.

If the values of one term increase as those of another decrease then consider their product.

To see them in action, consider how Bacon.1 derived Kepler's third law of planetary motion. This states that the cube of a planet's distance from the Sun is proportional to the square of its period. Stated in the form that Bacon.1 would understand it is: that: $D^3/P^2$ is constant, where $D$ is the distance and $P$ is the period. The account that follows is taken from a book, written by Simon and his co-workers, which describes their research. The text in italics are the processes that Bacon.1 uses to discover scientific laws. First the program prompts the user for data.

*When planet is A*
    *What is P?*          Answer: 1.0
    *What is D?*          Answer: 1.0

*When planet is B*
    *What is P?*          Answer: 8.0
    *What is D?*          Answer: 4.0

*When planet is C*
    *What is P?*          Answer: 27.0
    *What is D?*          Answer: 9.0

*D increases with P so I'll consider their ratio.*
*I'll define Term-1 as the ratio of D and P [D/P].*

This is an example of the second heuristic being applied. The distance and the period have been discovered to increase together, so the new concept *Term-1* has been defined as their ratio. Now the values of this new term are calculated:

| When D is: | 1.0 | 4.0 | 9.0 |
|---|---|---|---|
| and P is: | 1.0 | 8.0 | 27.0 |
| Term-1 is: | 1.0 | 0.5 | 0.333 |

*D increases as Term-1 decreases so I'll consider their product*
*I'll define Term-2 as the product of D and Term-1 $(D*(D/P)) = D^2/P$.*

| When D is: | 1.0 | 4.0 | 9.0 |
|---|---|---|---|
| and P is: | 1.0 | 8.0 | 27.0 |
| Term-2 is: | 1.0 | 2.0 | 3.0 |

*Term-1 increases as Term-2 decreases so I'll consider their product.*
*I'll define Term-3 as the product of Term-1 and Term-2 $(D/P)(D^2/P) = D^3/P^2$*

The third heuristic has been applied twice. Two more concepts have been defined: Term-2 as $D^2/P$ and Term-3 as $D^3/P^2$. Bacon.1 continues:

| When D is: | 1.0 | 4.0 | 9.0 |
|---|---|---|---|
| and P is: | 1.0 | 8.0 | 27.0 |
| Term-3 is: | 1.0 | 1.0 | 1.0 |

The first heuristic applies: the term $D^3/P^2$ has a constant value over all three planets.

This is rather an artificial example. The law itself is relatively trivial to discover, and the data gave a clean fit. However, the successors to Bacon.1 were much more sophisticated and rediscovered many more complicated laws.

Simon's work looks very old-fashioned in artificial intelligence terms. The history of artificial intelligence is split into two phases, each involves two schools of thought: the cognitive psychologists who want to use the computer as a laboratory to understand our psychological processes, and the tool builders who are more concerned with building intelligent artefacts, irrespective of whether they are based on any cognitive theories.

In the early days of artificial intelligence it was the former who dominated; scientists such as Simon were interested in human problem solving and attempted to model the processes using computer programs. In recent times, from the late 1970s onwards, it is the artefact builders who have come to the fore. The reason for this is simple: the cognitive psychologists set themselves large research goals. Consequently, they often experienced failure in the short term. The stress in research funding from the late 1970s has, in both the United Kingdom and the United States, been on research that could lead very quickly to the development of products. Consequently, when the prime example of an artificial intelligence product , the expert system, was brought to the attention of the Western world by the Japanese there was a shift in funding towards the artefact builders, with the consequence of a drift of workers away from the big issues.

Simon's work on scientific discovery is, in this sense, rather old-fashioned. His stress is always on mimicking the human expert. He has a very simple view of the cognitive processes that are involved in activities such as problem solving and vision. What he is saying is that the best scientists use a relatively simple reasoning process that can easily be modelled by a computer. His case is, as yet, not proven. However, it would be interesting to see what his program would make of real experimental data, where no laws have yet been discovered. To date, the Bacon programs have not discovered any new laws.

The two methods of computer learning that I have described in this chapter encapsulate the current dilemma of artificial intelligence. Quinlan's technique is grossly computational and does not owe allegiance to any branch of cognitive psychology. No artificial intelligence researcher would claim that the techniques presented in this chapter reflect the processes that occur in the human brain. Simon's method is claimed to be based on the fact that you can model human problem solving by means of sets of production rules that were discussed in Chapter 6.

Quinlan's method works well in domains where the factors that are identified can be quantified and are relatively few in number. Simon's method, since it promises to model human processes, could be capable of learning to a much deeper degree than Quinlan's technique. The next ten years should be crucial for artificial intelligence research. It is now almost an undergraduate project to build an expert system which has a few hundred rules. However, to build a system that has thousands of rules is a major undertaking, an undertaking that seems to be extremely difficult using the conventional technique of interviewing a human expert. The only solution seems to be the use of learning programs such as the ones described above. However, it is still an open question which type should be used.

Some clues could be gained from a field that has traditionally been a test-bed for ideas in artificial intelligence: chess. The reason that researchers have chosen chess is that it is a limited world, with a well-defined set of rules, in which human problem solving occurs. Current chess programs are based on a brute-force approach to game playing. What they do is to look at the chess board decide on a series of possible moves, then look at a number of moves that the opponent can make in response to each possible move, then look at the number of moves that the computer can make in response to these moves, and so on.

For each set of computer move, opponent move, computer move, opponent move ... the computer calculates how well it has fared. It produces a figure that gives the goodness of its position. For example, if the computer has lost a number of pieces during the set of moves, then the figure will be low; similarly, if one of the computer's pieces is trapped, then again the figure will be low. At the end of this process the computer searches for the best set of moves that will give a high value of advantage. It will then select the first of these moves for itself.

Now, this technique does not mimic the human chess player. Experiments on chess grandmasters seem to indicate that it is not the computational power of such players that is important, but their pattern-recognition powers. However, computers that use this grossly computational approach to chess have achieved some remarkable results. For example, in the early 1980s the grandmaster, David Levy, lost a speed chess game to the program CHESS 4.6, which was developed at the Northwestern University in the United States. After his defeat Levy stated that the program was better than 99.5% of all chess players.

Attempts to use techniques that are claimed to be close to those used by humans have had very limited success indeed. The majority of this work has been carried out using production rules, and has been relatively successful in the end-game phase when a few chess pieces remain on the board.

The evidence from chess seems to suggest that a computational approach may be the successful one to adopt when building learning programs. However, one warning is in order. Chess playing is still relatively simple compared with a number of human activities. For example, even in the area of game playing it is much easier to write chess-playing programs, than it is to write programs for the Oriental game of Go, where there are many more choices open to the player. Indeed, the Go programs that have been written have been quite disappointing.

So, the stage we have reached with machine learning is that it is still in its early days. All the work that has been carried out has been confined to limited domains where the factors are simple. However, it seems to be the only solution to building large expert systems containing thousands of rules. The stark choice now facing researchers is whether to use the computational powers of the machine or look to the human being.

# References

1.    The paper describing the technique is: Learning Efficient Classification Procedures and their Application to Chess End Games, R. Quinlan, in *Machine Learning: An Artificial Intelligence Approach*, Palo Alto, Calif.: Tioga Publishing. 1983.

2.    Finding Rules in Data, B. Thompson and W. Thompson, *Byte*, **11**, 2. 1986.

3.    *Scientific Discovery, Computational Explorations of the Creative Process*, P. Langley, H. Simon, G. Bradshaw, and J. Zytkow, Cambridge, Mass.: MIT Press. 1987.

# 10

# Ultra-reliable software and the mail order programmer

There are now large numbers of applications where faults in both hardware and software cannot be tolerated. Typical applications can be found in the areas of process monitoring, avionics, and hospital systems: a mistake by a program in sensing an overheating chemical reactor, or in injecting too much insulin into a diabetic's blood stream, would almost invariably have catastrophic results. Because of a massive increase in life-critical applications, a number of hardware companies have invested heavily in developing hardware systems that have an exceptionally high reliability. For example, the American computer manufacturers, Tandem, have become a highly successful hardware company through developing and marketing their non-stop systems based on hardware redundancy. Unfortunately, while high-reliability systems can now achieve very impressive mean times between failure, there still remains one major problem: software. No matter how reliable a hardware system is, if the software that runs on that computer is deficient, then potentially, catastrophic errors will occur.

Almost invariably, software errors occur because the designer of a system has forgotten a special case in the data being processed, or forgotten the effect of a number of actions that only occur very infrequently. Many such errors remain undetected until actual use; for a safety-critical system these can be disastrous. A recent example of such an error occurred during the firing of a new air-to-air missile from a fighter plane. The release mechanism for the missile closed before the missile had time to clear the plane and, suddenly, the pilot discovered that he had acquired an extra, rather unstable jet engine. The plane crashed in an unpopulated area; luckily, the pilot was able to use his ejector seat.

There are two approaches to increasing software reliability. The first involves the use of mathematics as a medium for specification. In Chapter 4 I discussed how a system can be specified in terms of mathematics and then designed and implemented, with each stage in the development process being mathematically validated. The proponents of so-called formal methods argue that there are major problems with current specification and design notations such as English: that they suffer from ambiguity, lack of clarity, and verbosity, and that these properties militate against specification and design errors being detected during early development.

The formal methods approach takes the view that the majority of errors can be detected by using notations of a more exact nature. A number of practitioners would argue that this represents a view of the software developer as a perfect being: that no matter what notation is used during the software project, there will always be errors committed and, consequently, methods need to be devised that enable a software system to tolerate these errors.

The major approaches to software tolerance that are being adopted are directly borrowed from the hardware community. All the techniques currently used rely on the type of redundancy employed in highly reliant systems where dual processors, memories, and backing storage units provide a high-integrity environment for hardware fault tolerance. Current software fault tolerance techniques are based on software redundancy. A simple way of implementing software redundancy in a highly reliable system is shown in Figure 10.1.

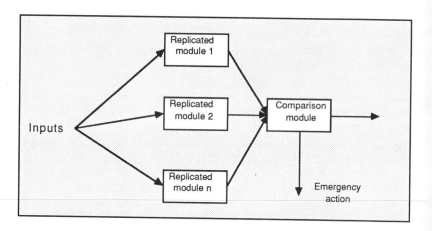

**Figure 10.1.**

It consists of a number of modules that have been independently developed: a specification of each module is given to a number of programmers who do not communicate, and who implement the module using their own ideas of what processing should occur and what data is required. During the operation of a system containing such modules, each module carries out the same function, and a comparison module checks the results from each one. If an error occurs, then some emergency action is taken. The comparison module can carry out the monitoring of the outputs from the replicated modules in a number of ways. First, the outputs from each module can be compared against each other and some voting mechanism used: if the majority of the modules agree what the result should be, then the execution of the system is correct. A second approach involves the comparison module checking that each output is acceptable.

The second approach to software tolerance is exemplified by a method devised at the University of Newcastle.[1] Researchers have invented a technique that involves software developers using a programming concept known as a recovery block. This is a facility that enables the programmer to specify the use of a number of alternative modules, and also to write down the test that they have to pass if they are functioning correctly. An outline of a recovery block is shown below:

| | |
|---|---|
| ensure | *acceptance test* |
| by | *primary module* |
| else by | *alternate module 1* |
| . | |
| . | |
| else by | *alternate module n* |
| else | *error* |

Assume that a developer has produced a module in system for which he requires a high degree of confidence in correctness; for example, the flap control module in an airliner. He would insert the above lines into this program. *Acceptance test* is a test that checks that the output from a module is sensible, for example, in a system for managing and predicting foreign exchange transactions, the acceptance test might check that a predicted foreign exchange movement is in a valid range. *Primary module, alternate module 1, alternate module 2*, etc., are different implementations of a module derived from a common specification. These modules would normally be developed by a number of separate programmers.

With this form of error-tolerant computing, before the modules above are entered, the state of the software system is saved. *Primary module* is executed and it is checked by the acceptance test to see whether it is valid. If it is, the system continues executing. However, if the acceptance test fails then a serious error has occurred in the primary module, usually because it has been designed or programmed badly. In this case the system is restored to the position it was at before the primary module was executed. What then happens is that *alternate module 1* is executed and its output is checked. If the output is valid then the system continues executing: if not, the system state is restored and the next module is tried. This process is continued until a module executes correctly or an error is signalled.

This technique was recently tested on a realistic system that was intended for a naval command and control system.[2] In one phase of the experiment, the command and control software was modified by replacing some versions of modules by modules that were developed by inexperienced staff, and in which it was expected there would be a higher density of errors. During the experiment 222 failures due to bugs could have occurred. However, only 57 actual errors surfaced, because the software had become so fault tolerant that alternative modules were used when the errors were discovered. In fact these figures could have been much better. The system software and support software used in the experiment should have been of the highest reliability. For a number of reasons this was not the case. If it had been, only 20 errors would have surfaced.

These are remarkable figures. If the software was produced in a production environment, without incompletely developed and tested modules, then it seems very likely that the system would have tolerated all the errors that would have occurred.

Another technique is known as N-version programming.[3] It is similar to the recovery block scheme. However, it differs in one respect: all the versions of a module are executed in parallel. Their outputs are examined and the outcome that occurs most often is taken as the correct one. This technique is the same as that used in the hardware employed in the space shuttle. It is being extensively evaluated by NASA and the American Navy, and is based on research carried out at the University of California at Los Angeles.

Software reliability will become big business. The market for high-reliability applications software is increasing as microcomputers become smaller and smaller, and more and more demands are made by customers for life-critical applications. However, the computing industry is now realizing that ultra-reliable hardware is not the sole answer. A hardware system can have no fault in it at all but, because of errors in its software, it can be virtually useless. Tandem made large profits in the 1970s and 1980s through being the first in the field with reliable hardware. There are similar prizes for the first software company that does the same with reliable software.

Researchers into software reliability have pointed out that a number of spin-offs from this research are possible. Techniques such as the recovery block could enable more relaxed quality assurance standards to be used on software projects, because of the increase in software fault tolerance that would occur. This means that the overhead costs in a highly controlled professional programming environment would be drastically reduced, since many programmers would be able to work at home and utilize low-cost computing facilities. There would be less of a requirement for activities such as design walkthroughs and test reviews.

Similarly, the use of software-tolerant techniques might enable the growing number of hobbyists to be employed on software projects. Currently, we have the paradox that there is an increasing programming skills shortage, together with an burgeoning number of hobbyists with relatively sophisticated design and programming skills. The use of software fault tolerance would resolve the paradox, and could enable hobbyists to be employed on a mail order basis, where a central facility would contract out multiple versions of individual modules together with the acceptance test that each module would need to pass.

Finally, these techniques may rebound back into the hardware area, from where they were originally taken. The complexity of modern VLSI circuits increases by an order of magnitude every few years. We now have chips with 500 000 gates available and one million gates will soon be the norm. Because of this increase in size, hardware developers are now experiencing the same type of errors that software designers have encountered during the 1970s and 1980s. Design duplication in hardware would enable many of the errors that would be committed, because of gate complexity, to be tolerated.

## References

1.  A readable description of the Newcastle method is contained in the paper: Design Fault Tolerance in Practical Systems, written by Tom Anderson. It is contained in a book of related papers on high integrity systems: *Software Reliability, Achievement and Assessment*, B. Littlewood (Ed.), Oxford, U.K.: Blackwell Scientific. 1987.

2.  Software Fault Tolerance: an Evaluation, T. Anderson *et al.*, *IEEE Transactions on Software Engineering*, **11**, 12. 1985.

3.  An account of this work can be found in: Design Diversity — The Challenge of the Eighties, *Digest of the 12th International Symposium on Fault Tolerant Computing*. Santa Monica.

# 11

# Too little time and too little memory

The growth in computing power over the last twenty years has made us optimistic about the capabilities of computers. We now think that no matter how complex or how large a problem we have, we can write a computer program to solve it. However, the last fifteen years have seen the emergence of disturbing evidence that there is an upper limit to the power of the computer. Problems exist that are not only incapable of being solved by present-day computers; but are also incapable of being solved by computers that are the products of the wildest imaginings of science-fiction writers. Even if one could build a computer with millions of processors, and massive stores with speeds rivalling that of light, there are problems that are so intrinsically difficult that they cannot be programmed efficiently.

Two years ago I came across one of these problems. I was trying to develop a computer program that examined a series of software designs and selected the best one from a large number of possible designs. The program seemed to work quite well when it examined a hundred designs. It produced an answer in about five seconds. When it came to a thousand designs it took about a minute. However, when it had to examine ten thousand designs it took well over an hour. Since the program was only practical if it could process millions of designs, I despaired.

These hard problems exhibit an explosive growth in computer time or memory requirements as their size increases. The computer time for the solution to one of these problems is shown below. It is known as the graph colouring problem and involves assigning colours to the lines joining a set of points. The details of the problem are not important; what is important is the massive growth of computer time used to solve the problem. The left column represents the number of points processed. The right column represents the time, in milliseconds, required to solve the problem by a computer.

| | |
|---|---|
| 1 | 1 |
| 2 | 4 |
| 3 | 27 |
| 4 | 256 |
| . | . |
| 10 | 10 000 000 000 |

The solution to the graph colouring problem for ten points would take over 115 days of computer time. This would be much longer than the mean time between failures for most modern computers! For practical problem sizes of more than a hundred points the computer time required would exceed the known future life of the universe!

Prior to the 1970s computing researchers knew of the existence of a few problems that could not be computerized. However, in 1971 the study of computationally difficult problems was put on a mathematically respectable footing; it lead to the discovery of thousands more difficult problems.

Stephen Cooke, an American computer scientist, in a remarkable mathematical *tour-de-force*,[1] showed that all known computationally difficult problems could be characterized mathematically. Cooke called these problems *NP complete*. He provided a mathematical framework that enabled computer scientists to look at a new problem and discover whether it was NP complete. Cooke didn't provide a proof that NP complete problems were impossible to solve. However, the last decade has seen the emergence of a large amount of empirical evidence that supports the conjecture that if a problem is NP complete, then no efficient computer program can be written to solve it. Many thousands of problems have been shown to be NP complete and nobody has yet been able to write an efficient computer program for any of them.

The study of NP complete problems involves highly abstract mathematics. However, the problems themselves are highly practical. They arise in areas such as electronic circuit design, computer networks, and fluid mechanics. They also include many problems in artificial intelligence. Indeed, artificial intelligence has been described as the approximate solution of NP complete problems using knowledge

One of the most important applications of NP completeness occurs in cryptography. The availability of high-speed computers has rendered obsolete many of the ciphers that have been the workhorses of the security and armed forces. Moreover, the increased use of computers in areas such as banking and insurance has also increased the demands on the cryptographer.

One promising technique for coding messages is known as public key encryption. It is efficient and extremely secure. Each user of a public key cryptosystem has two keys. The first key is known as a public key; this is known by all the users of a communication system. The second key is known as a private key; it is known only by the user. If I wanted to send a message to a colleague I would first find his public key. This would then be used to scramble the message so that it would be undecipherable. To read this message my colleague would use his private key for decoding.

The mathematics of public key cryptosystems is such that an intruder who wished to read a message would have to solve an NP complete problem. In many public key systems this problem is the factorization of a 200-digit number. With current methods of factorization this would take millions of years, even using the current fastest computers. It is hardly surprising that many of the papers on NP completeness are classified!

Another NP problem connected with computers is based on the travelling salesman problem. The problem is abstracted in Figure 11.1. It shows a number of cities connected by routes, each of which has a cost associated with it; think of the cost as rail fares, or the mileage between the cities. The solution to the travelling salesman problem is to work out an itinerary that takes a salesman to all the cities, but which, at the same time, minimizes the cost of the journey.

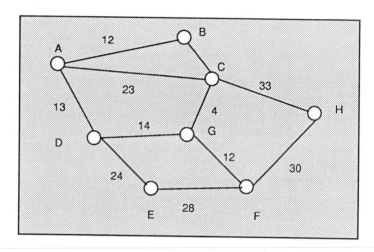

**Figure 11.1.** The travelling salesman problem.

The computer-related problem based on this involves the scheduling of resources in a computer system. Assume a large computer centre has a number of programs to run. Each of these programs requires different resources: a compiler, certain stored files, and a quantity of main memory. Each set of resources is known as a configuration. The switching of the computer system from one configuration to another configuration has a cost associated with it. Usually the cost is expressed in terms of the lost amount of computer time that is needed to switch from one configuration to another. A computer centre manager wants to order the programs that are to be executed by his computer so that they will minimize his costs. Now this problem does not look very much like the travelling salesman problem. In fact it is exactly the same if you substitute configurations for cities and conversion cost for mileage or rail fare.

Because of the importance of NP completeness a massive amount of research has been carried out into the efficient solution of these computationally difficult problems. There are two strands to this research. The first is highly speculative: a major feature of Cooke's theory of NP completeness is that if you can find an efficient solution to just *one* NP complete problem then you have demonstrated that an efficient program exists for every NP complete problem in existence. The search for one efficient program is the major research problem in computer science. It ranks with mathematical blockbusters such as Fermat's Last Theorem and the Riemann conjecture. An efficient solution to an NP complete problem would be a major landmark in computing.

The second strand of research is more realistic. It involves devising solutions to NP complete problems that give an approximate result, in a relatively short time. For example, when I discovered that my program for finding the best design out of a set of designs was NP complete, the next task that I set myself was to develop a program that found a design that was within 5% of the best design, and which didn't occupy my computer for days on end. The search for approximate solutions to NP complete problems is a major intellectual exercise. A number of general-purpose tactics can be used to solve a small subset of problems; however, for the majority of the NP complete problems in existence, the researcher has only his intellect to help him.

There are also major problems with demonstrating that you have obtained an efficient solution. In order to do this you require large sets of data together with the exact result from this data. The result is needed in order to check that your program is correct. Now, since the problems to be solved are NP complete you cannot extract this result automatically, it has to be calculated by hand. For anything but the most trivial sets of data this is quite an undertaking. So much resource is required that the test sets for programs that determine approximate solutions to NP complete problems are usually inadequate to give much confidence in the program.

Many NP complete problems are deceptively simple. Two are described below. If you want to write your name into the computing history books then all you need do is construct an efficient program to solve them. The first problem is known as the integer partition problem. You are given a series of integers and your task is to develop a program that decides whether the integers can be split up into two sets whose sums are equal. For example, the set

$$8,8,9,7,3,4,1,2,10,17,9,13,1,2,4,6$$

can be partitioned into the sets

$$13,17,8,7,3,4 \quad \text{and} \quad 9,1,2,10,9,8,1,2,4,6$$

each of which adds up to 52, while the set

$$7,9,3,4$$

cannot be partitioned. Although this problem looks fairly abstract it has many applications in the design of high-speed silicon chips. If you think you have an efficient program try it out on a hundred integers.

The second problem is one that occurs in transportation. It involves a series of commodities. Each commodity has a profit associated with it, together with a size. The aim is to develop a program that allocates some of the commodities to a lorry, so that the lorry is filled or almost filled, and the profit is maximized. For example, assume the lorry has a size of 2000 cubic metres and the commodities have sizes of 100, 200, 300, 500, 800, 900, 1100, and 1300 cubic metres and an associated profit of 1, 3, 2, 5, 4, 2, 4, and 5 pounds. Then three possible loads are:

900 + 1100 cubic metres with a profit of 6 pounds
200 + 300 + 500 + 800 cubic metres with a profit of 14 pounds
100 + 200 + 300 + 500 + 900 cubic metres with a profit of 13 pounds

The aim is to write a program that maximizes the profit. Try it out on a hundred commodities! In order to discover whether you have an efficient solution to any NP complete problem, follow this procedure: first select a hundred sets of data. Start off with a small number of items of data, say, five items; make sure that your final set of data is substantial, say a thousand items. Then, run your program for each set of data and time how long it took. Plot the time against the number of items of data in each test set. If you have a steeply rising line such as the one shown in Figure 11.2, or have to wait an inordinate amount of time for your results, then your program is not efficient.

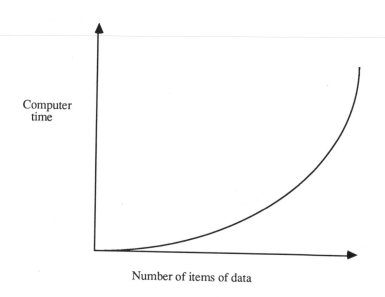

Number of items of data

Figure 11.2. The progress of an NP problem.

However, if your program run time only rises gradually, then feel you can award yourself the Nobel prize. You've solved one of the great problems of mathematics and destroyed a massive edifice that computer scientists have erected over the past fifteen years.[2]

I would be quite depressed by such a discovery. I find it strangely reassuring that no matter how big our computer become, no matter how efficient our programming methods, there will be problems that are impossible to solve.

## References

1. The Complexity of Theorem Proving Procedures, S. Cooke, *Proceedings of the 3rd Annual ACM Symposium on the Theory of Computing.* 1971.

2. If you have a good knowledge of mathematics, the clearest exposition of NP completeness is in the book: *The Design and Analysis of Computer Algorithms*, A. Aho, J. Hopcroft, and J. Ullman, Reading, Mass.: Addison-Wesley. 1974. Be warned, however, NP completeness is not a subject for the faint-hearted!

# 12

# Reusable software — the false frontier

One of the useful properties of engineered products is the degree to which their components can be reused. Nowadays, it is quite common for an alternator for one car to be used in another car, and for aero-engines to be used across disparate airliner models. It is not surprising, then, that with the increasing emphasis on the development of software as an engineering process, that researchers are turning their attention to the concept that software should be reused. If a major part of the software production process consisted of slotting prefabricated chunks of software together, then large gains in software productivity would follow. A number of American companies, particularly in the commercial data-processing field, report that from 40% to 60% of the actual program code of their systems is capable of being repeated in more than one application. This chapter explores how far we have reached in developing techniques that respond to these figures.

Surprisingly, there are a number of examples of the successful use of reusable software dating from the 1960s. Probably the best involves the use of subroutines. A subroutine is a collection of program statements that can be written, given a name, and used a number of times in a program, just by quoting the name. Often, inside a program the same processing is required at a number of places; instead of writing the same section of code each time that it was required, a developer would write a subroutine and insert its name at the points in the program where it was needed.

For example, a system for administering bank accounts may need to look up customer details in a number of places. Say, in checking a balance, or in responding to an over-the-counter request for the last series of transactions of the account. A subroutine to extract these details from the customer files would be written and inserted wherever it was needed. The use of subroutines produced savings on two fronts: first, it saved computer memory; second, it saved the programmer a considerable amount of time.

In the early days of computing it was discovered that subroutines were not only useful inside the same system but could be used in other systems. For example, a subroutine that might be used to sort names in alphabetical order would find use in systems that provided management information for bank managers, administered computerized mailing lists, and organized class timetables in a university.

The area where this idea of subroutines being reused has been most successful is in a branch of mathematics known as numerical analysis. This is the study of computational procedures that are used in solving numerical problems. A typical problem that is solved by numerical analysts is the solution of extremely large sets of equations involving hundreds of unknowns. Such sets of equations arise in areas such as civil engineering during the calculation of stress in concrete structures, and in electrical engineering during the calculation of currents in large circuits. Numerical analysts have developed extremely efficient programs for the solution of such problems .

These programs are often needed in a wide variety of applications; two have already been mentioned above, other applications include medicine, aero-engineering, automotive engineering, and nuclear physics. It was obvious, even during the early days of computing, that a subroutine needed to solve numerical equations in, say, civil engineering needed little, if any, modification when used in a different environment. Consequently, large libraries of such subroutines have been built up and are used by research and development staff the world over.

In many cases the programs that such staff needed to develop consisted of a few lines to input numerical data from a computer terminal or a file, use a pre-written subroutine, and output the results to a printer. Probably the most famous of these libraries is British and is administered by the Numerical Algorithms Group at Oxford. It contains hundreds of subroutines that can solve virtually every type of numerical problem known. The vast majority of scientist using this library never carry out any modification to the subroutines, they just slot them into their programs.

Subroutine libraries have proved exceptionally useful in areas that use mathematics. However, they have only proved suitable for tasks that are very similar. For example, one of the standard subroutines found in a numerical library is one that solves massive sets of equations. The user of such a system provides a set of numbers which characterize the equations, and a solution is produced. These numbers could represent stress values in a nuclear reactor, values of resistances in electrical networks, and flows in an oil pipeline. Because only numbers are required in each application, the subroutine can be reused time and time again.

In contrast to this, consider a subroutine that counts the frequency with which numbers less than a hundred occur in a stream of data. It is much more difficult to reuse this subroutine, say, in a data-processing application where a count of the number of employees who have surnames starting with A may be required. What would be required is to modify the original subroutine to carry out the required task. As soon as modification takes place you start losing the main benefit of reusability: that it saves you resources; the programmer who has to carry out the modification needs to understand the function of the subroutine by reading the program code, a task that is often as time-consuming as developing the subroutine from scratch.

Another example of software reuse technology that is currently employed is table-driven software. The idea behind table-driven software is that you have a general-purpose system that can be parameterized towards different applications. Each time a new application was required a table of values would be changed that reflected the application. A concrete example will make this clear.

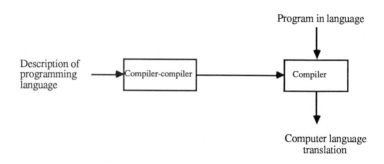

**Figure 12.1.** The compiler-compiler.

Perhaps the best example of a table-driven software system is the compiler-compiler. A compiler is a program that translates a programming language into the language of the computer. A compiler-compiler is a program that, as its output, produces a compiler. It does this more quickly than the normal route of developing the compiler from scratch. A schematic that describes its operation is shown in Figure 12.1. The user of a compiler-compiler first produces a mathematical description of the language for which a compiler is needed. This is then incorporated in a table that is used by the compiler-compiler.

The compiler-compiler then takes this description and produces, as its output, a compiler. This can then be used to process programs in the language the user was interested in and carry out the translation into machine language. Research into compiler-compilers was a very glamorous and well-funded research topic in the 1960s. These days it is a very quiet area indeed. There are two reasons for this. First, in the 1960s developing a compiler was a black art and, consequently, consumed a large amount of resource; therefore, the prospect of being able to produce one just by writing a mathematical description was very tempting. Today we know much more about the theory of writing compilers: one of the standard third-year exercises during a computer science course is for an undergraduate to produce a compiler for a small language.

The second reason for compiler-compiler research being a backwater is that the process of building up the description of a language in a table proved much more difficult than many researchers thought. Although compiler-compilers have been a relative failure, the technique that they employ is finding use in many of the reusability methods that are being used, and being researched, today. Indeed, one of the most practical tool-sets for reusability is based on it, and can be found inside the UNIX operating system

UNIX is, first and foremost, a collection of programs that administers the resources of microcomputers and minicomputers. It shares out storage space for user files and also shares out time on a computer to the large number of users who might be using the computer simultaneously. However, what has made UNIX so popular is a set of table-based software tools that enable reuse.[1] A typical tool which is part of every UNIX system is AWK. This is a processor that carries out pattern matching. It enables the user to develop programs for applications such as report generation, where records are extracted from a file and displayed, the extraction being based on some of the characteristics of the data stored in them. For example AWK might enable a bank to develop a program that scanned customers' accounts which are in credit, or customers' accounts that have had no transactions logged against them for a number of years.

Another state-of-the-art technique, based on table-driven technology, is the application generator. Such generators are usually found in commercial data processing. What they provide are high-level facilities for generating programs and for manipulating files. The description of the programs and the files is specified in a table format. Probably the best example of a modern application generator is QBE/OBE,[1] an office automation system developed at IBM, which features built-in facilities for word-processing, electronic mail, graphics, and general data processing. Objects known to the IBM system include letters, forms, charts, graphs, and audio documents.

One futuristic technique that holds out some promise is based on the transformational methods described in Chapter 8. Researchers at the Argonne National Laboratory in Illinois have been using program transformation methods to convert programs written in an inefficient programming language into more efficient languages.[3]

Their work was necessary because they were faced with a large program, written in the artificial intelligence language LISP, that consumed large quantities of memory and processor power. The program was required to be moved to a less-powerful computer that did not possess any LISP software. The complexity of the program was such that reprogramming by hand would have introduced errors and made the process economically infeasible.

The researchers used a program transformation system called TAMPR to carry out the transformation from LISP to the widely available scientific programming language FORTRAN. Not only was this process totally error-free, but it gave rise to a version of the LISP software that was considerably more efficient.

This is still not a full blown application of program transformation. The conversion was not from a specification into a program, as described in Chapter 8, but from a program written in one programming language to a program in another language. However, it uses many of the techniques that lie at the heart of automatic programming theory. It is important in two respects.

First, it provides encouragement to the flagging automatic programming community. Few practical results have yet to emerge from their work, and a number of groups will soon begin to face grant renewals and the inevitable demand for end-products. The Argonne work is the first practical application of automatic programming ideas.

Second, it enables developers who use inefficient programming languages to produce computer programs that are relatively efficient in terms of computer resources. Such programs normally occur in artificial intelligence applications such as robotics and computer vision, where heavy computational demands are placed on software. Any inefficiencies in software show up very quickly, with poor response time and limited capabilities. The Argonne work holds out hope for struggling researchers in artificial intelligence who are attempting to squeeze every millisecond out of their overburdened computers.

Equally futuristic work is being carried out in a number of American universities on using specifications and designs for reusability. One of the features of the software engineering process is that as you progress through a development project, the description of the software that you are producing gets more and more detailed, and the choices open to the developer become more and more closed. A good system specification should give the developer as much choice as possible, it should leave free any of his implementation options, for example whether to use one form of data storage as against another ; a system design has closed down the options, since the structure of the system has been defined in terms of modules; and finally, the program code leaves no choices to the developer, everything is fixed in clay. The further back in the software project you go the more scope you get for reuse. As an example, consider the problem of sorting a set of data in some particular order. At the programming language stage you have to specify the exact nature of the data that is to be sorted, for example whether it is numeric or alphabetic, and you have to specify the ordering rule that is used to compare the items during sorting. A design does not have to describe such items of concern in such detail. For example, the text below is the detailed design of a module for sorting a set of data in a file into order, albeit inefficiently. It carries out the sorting by repeatedly finding the lowest item in a file, and then moving it further forward in the file.

```
SORT (file)
Set i to one
REPEAT
     Find an item in file after the ith item, with the
     lowest value
     Interchange it with the ith item in the file
     Increment i by one
UNTIL all the items have been examined
```

Notice that this design leaves a number of choices free. For example, it does not specify the nature of the data, nether does it describe the exact criteria for selecting the lowest item in the file. For example, it could be the lowest numerically, the lowest alphabetically, or the choice based it could even have made on values of a number of items of data in each record. For example, the sorting could be on a name, with people having the same name being sorted by address within name. The point is, that a document that is produced early in the software project is potentially more useful than program code because it leaves a number of implementation choices free.

A large amount of academic research is being applied to the idea that one can take a document such as a detailed design, system design, or even a functional specification, and then use that as the basis for generating a number of implementations of program code that reflect the document, but that are oriented towards different applications. Normally the documents that are processed are much more exact than the detailed design presented above; in fact, mathematics is the only medium that is really capable of the precision required for describing reusable software.

Probably the most impressive piece of work that is based on the idea of using designs and specifications as the basis for reuse was carried out by researchers at Harvard University.[4] The concept the researchers have invented is known as an abstract program; in many ways this is similar to a detailed design. They have developed a system that processes an abstract program and, by means of a series of transformations, produces a program that is targeted towards one particular application.

Software reuse is often hailed as the next frontier, particularly by those who are looking for grant support. However, one of the most surprising aspects of software reuse is how much occurs at the present time in industry. I have already mentioned two examples of popular techniques of reuse: the subroutine library and UNIX. Both are extensively used within commercial environments. There are many more examples of reuse being employed in industry. Probably the most startling example is the spreadsheet.

When the history of computing is written I am sure that historians who examine the last twenty years of software development will point to the spreadsheet as a significant step forward. Essentially, a spreadsheet is, in its raw form, a grid of squares into which numbers and words can be inserted. The user of a spreadsheet system can then manipulate these squares, for example, by adding up columns or rows. In this way accountants can easily build up balance sheets, civil engineers can keep track of materials, and the householder can maintain financial records.

Spreadsheets have become a major success story, the reason, of course — and it is true of any really successful software idea — is that it provides a framework that mirrors the way in which the user works. For example, accountants actually think in terms of rows and columns of figures. The subsequent history of the spreadsheet has included the addition of programming languages and facilities for the graphic display of charts. Now, with these additions they have become an excellent medium for reusability. Using the programming languages associated with these spreadsheets, sophisticated applications can be developed very quickly. As I write I have in front of me a catalogue of packages for a wide variety of businesses, all generated by a remarkably powerful spreadsheet system developed by the Microsoft Corporation; it includes software for estate agents, travel agents, civil engineers, management accountants, and cost accountants. Although one can criticize the languages that have been grafted onto spreadsheets, it is still a fact of life that they are enabling a large degree of reuse in the commercial data-processing arena.

Another example in the reusable software revolution are the file packages and simple data-processing systems that are now coming onto the market. I use one of these packages; it enables me to store records about my business activities, to retrieve records according to some particular criterion and define forms layouts, reminder letters, and mailing labels. For example, it allows me to examine a list of papers published in computing, select those papers that have been published in a particular journal, and in a particular year on a particular topic.

Now spreadsheets and file packages are mostly of use to individuals, for example, managers and academics like myself. However, there is increasing evidence that a relatively low-tech approach to reusability can achieve major gains in productivity. At the Raytheon company, a major American defence firm, reusability has become a fact of life.[5]

In 1976 the management at Raytheon initiated a study of the program code produced by their development teams. The results that they obtained were startling. They discovered that between 40 and 60% of the code that they examined was redundant and could be reused. In order to take advantage of this they developed a series of texts known as logic structures. These were essentially skeletons of program code, which were the same no matter what program they were used in, and contained gaps where program statements for the application being developed could fit.

All a programmer at Raytheon needed to do when building a system, was to identify what logic structures were needed, plug them into the system and then add the code that was system-specific. This is not a sophisticated approach. Yet, the gains that they achieved were larger than the gains reported with other techniques such as formal methods and prototyping. The staff at Raytheon employ approximately 60% of reusable code in their development. This has lead to a 50% increase in productivity. A similar approach has been adopted by IBM for system software: the programs that are used to keep a computer running. Developers at IBM have reported that reuse rates of 50% were achieved and an order of magnitude of improvement in software errors was obtained.[6] This is one advantage of reusable software that tends to get forgotten: that well-used modules tend to have been thoroughly tested and very rarely give rise to errors.

Of all the techniques described in this book, software reuse seems to have had the most industrial penetration. While there is valuable work being done on research into specifying mathematically how reusable modules are described and on using transformational techniques to generate various concrete instances of a program from a common specification, my overwhelming impression is of a false frontier. Relatively simple managerial methods, together with the exceptionally good table-driven software being written for computers such as the Apple Macintosh, have resulted in the major gains, and that gains from further work will be marginal.

## References

1.  The scope that Unix offers for reusability is described in: The Unix System and Software Reusability, B. Kernighan, *IEEE Transactions on Software Engineering*, **10**, 5. 1984.

2.  QBE/OBE: A language for Business Automation, M. Zloof, *Computer*, **14**. 1981.

3.  Program Reusability Through Program Transformation, J. Boyle and M. Muralidharan, *IEEE Transactions on Software Engineering*, **10**, 5. 1984.

4.  Reusability Through Program Transformations, T. Standish, *IEEE Transactions on Software Engineering*, **10**, 5. 1984.

5.  Software Engineering with Reusable Designs and Code, R. G. Lanergan and C. A. Grasso, *IEEE Transactions on Software Engineering*, **10**, 5. 1984.

6.  Software Reuse Through Building Blocks, G. E. Kaiser and D. Garlan, *IEEE Software*, **7**. 1987.

# 13

# Cleaning out the garage

Ask any programmer what is the most unpopular task that he has to carry out and, next to cleaning out the garage, he would probably say testing. Of all the activities in the software project, testing is probably the most boring, repetitive, and error-prone. Apart from staff who enjoy arcane, convoluted problems, the common view of developmental staff is that software testing is demeaning, and since it has little element of creativity it is an activity that really should be carried out by somebody else.

Before describing a number of advances that try to solve some of the problems of testing, it is worth briefly describing what it involves in an industrial project. The first time that the subject of testing appears in a project is just after the system specification has been written. This system specification will consist, for the most part, of details of what a system is to do. It is the base document for a software project, and one on which all subsequent activities depend. The developer has to process this document and devise a series of tests, known as the acceptance tests, which, when applied at the end of the project when the software has been completed, will demonstrate to the customer that the system meets its specification. This is an extremely time-consuming and difficult task: the system specification is often a large document occupying a number of volumes of text and, on anything but the smallest projects, can give rise to tens of thousands of individual tests. Once the acceptance tests have been completed they are agreed with the customer; they are then filed away to wait for the production of a full system.

The developer then designs the system in terms of modules. Each module, when designed, is then programmed. Once a module has been completely programmed it is then tested. This involves the programmer selecting test data that, when processed correctly, gives him confidence that the module meets its design. This is a process known as unit testing.

The next occurrence of testing is during the process of building up a system out of tested modules. A software developer does not throw together all the tested modules at once. The strategy he adopts is to gradually add modules to a partially built system, one or two at a time, until the whole system has been assembled. Each time that modules are added, the partially built system is tested. The main aim of these tests, known as integration tests, is to ensure that the interfaces between modules are correct; although occasionally integration testing also picks up errors that have not been discovered during unit testing.

Once a system has been built up the developer applies a subset of the acceptance tests to the software. These act as a final check that the system is behaving as it should; it usually avoids the embarrassment of the customer witnessing failed acceptance tests. Once the system tests are complete the software is installed in the environment in which it is to function, and the acceptance tests are applied.

Acceptance testing is a nerve-wracking process for the project manager. There will be many thousands of such tests, and if only one fails the customer can insist that after the fault that caused the failure has been rectified, the whole series of tests is carried out again. The reason for this is that in rectifying a fault the developer may have introduced other faults; the customer has every right in asking the developer to rerun every test to ensure that this has not happened.

This, then, is the process of testing. What problems does it suffer from? The first problem is fundamental: that testing discovers the presence of errors, but is never able to confirm their absence. No matter how thoroughly a software system is tested there is no guarantee that there are no residual errors. This is one of the major reasons given by the proponents of formal methods in favour of using mathematics on a software project ; it is a topic that was explored in Chapter 4.

The second problem is that testing is time-consuming and repetitive. For example, the process of unit testing consists of a seemingly endless cycle of deriving test data, executing a module, checking which parts of the module were exercised by the data, examining the outcome of the test, checking that it is correct, searching for the error, modifying the module to eliminate the error, and rerunning the test.

The third problem is a psychological one. A system is an artefact created by a team of software developers, a module is created by one programmer. In both cases the process of developing these objects is a long and arduous one, after which many programmers feel that what they have created is somehow a reflection of their own professionalism. This feeling of possession, akin to parenthood, prevents many members of a development team thoroughly testing a system. After all, an error is a reflection on their own competence. Consequently, systems tend to be tested less thoroughly than they should be.

One solution to the first problem, of the inability of testing to give total confidence in the correctness in a software system, has been dealt with at length in Chapter 4, in which the use of mathematics was described. All that needs to be said here is that formal methods of software development still have a long way to go before they become employed in industrial projects and, in any possible interregnum, it is worth ensuring that testing is carried out thoroughly. In fact, even if tomorrow there was a revolution in software development and mathematics was extensively used, then there would still be a need to test software, particularly during acceptance testing, when a customer wants a live demonstration of the running of a system, and does not want to be presented with hundreds of pages of mathematics.

The second problem is the repetitive nature of testing and the amount of resource that is consumed in deriving test data. It is this problem that has received the most attention from researchers over the past two decades; in particular, there has been a large amount of work on the automatic derivation of test data.

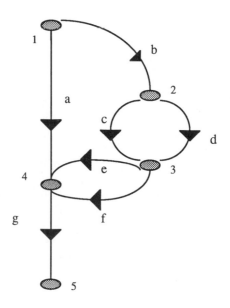

**Figure 13.1.** A program graph.

In order to understand how automatic test data generation can be carried out, it is first necessary to look again at the internal structure of computer programs. One representation, described in Chapter 1, is shown in Figure 13.1. It is known as a *program graph*. It shows the processing that occurs inside a small program or module. The lightly shaded ovals represent processing choices while the lines represent some processing that occurs. For example, the graph shown below might represent a small program for the stock control in a warehouse, which is used by a stock control clerk in allocating orders for items stored in the warehouse. For such a program, decision 2 might represent the processing choice that occurs in discovering whether a particular item is in stock; if the item is in stock, then the processing corresponding to line *c*, takes place and the part is allocated to a particular customer: if the item is not in stock, then the processing corresponding to line *d* takes place, and a message is printed that tells the stock control clerk that the item is out of stock.

The example that I have used is artificial: even small modules will contain many more lines and ovals. However, the principle behind representing a computer program as a series of ovals, and lines joining the ovals, still holds.

One of the main aims in carrying out testing is to ensure that the test data used covers as many decisions and processing lines as possible.

A developer can be assured that his test data is thorough if, when a program or module is tested, each individual processing branch is executed at least once. In the example above this means that test data has to be selected that results in branches $a, b, c, d, e, f, g$, being executed. In a computer program each branch represents some decision expressed in mathematics, for example branch 2, in the hypothetical stock control program, which tested whether there was any stock for an item might be written as:

```
IF stock >0 THEN
```

It is these decisions which are the key to research in automatic test data generation. There are now a number of successful systems for generating test data. A typical architecture for such a system is shown in Figure 13.2.

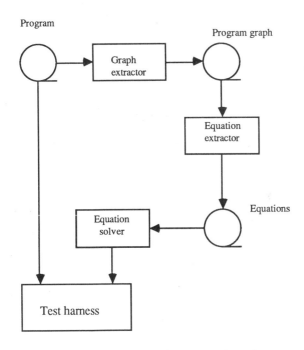

**Figure 13.2.** The architecture of an automatic testing system.

The system to be tested is first processed by a program known as a graph extractor. What this does is to extract the directed graph from the program under test, together with all the decisions in that program. This graph is then processed by an equation solver. This looks at all the decisions in the program graph, collects them together as a series of equations that have to be solved in order that test data should exercise all the processing parts of the program under test. It then solves the equations, and the solution is the data that is required for the program to be tested thoroughly. The program is then placed in a test harness, the data is channelled to it, and the program is executed and tested. During this process little human intervention is required.

A number of automatic test data generation systems have been developed.[1] The vast majority of such systems have been written for conventional programming languages such as FORTRAN and COBOL. The reason for this is that programs written in such languages contain decisions that, for the most part, are numerical in nature and give rise to equations containing numbers, which current software technology is able to solve.

One of the most interesting attempts at automatically generating test data involves a technique known as adaptive testing.[2] This attempts to examine the effectiveness of a test, and to derive data that will improve this effectiveness. The architecture of an adaptive test system is shown in Figure 13.3:

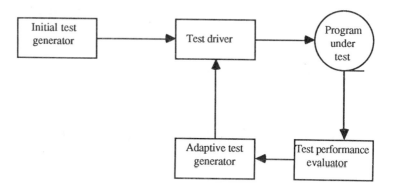

**Figure 13.3.** The architecture of an adaptive test system.

It consist of a number of components: an initial test generator that supplies the first set of test data; a test driver, which is a software module that feeds the test data to the program under test; a test performance evaluator that monitors how well a test has been performed; and an adaptive test generator that attempts to derive test data that increases the test effectiveness, and which uses information passed to it by the test performance evaluator in order to select the data.

The initial test data generator first supplies one set of test data. This is fed to the program under test by the test harness. The program is executed and the effectiveness of the test data is monitored by the performance evaluator. The effectiveness is then used to modify the test data in order to increase test effectiveness. The new test data is then fed to the program under test, which is executed again, and the cycle continues until the program has been effectively tested.

There are two ways of monitoring test effectiveness. The first is to check how many processing paths have been traversed. The second way is to insert correctness assertions inside the program that is to be tested. A correctness assertion is a small section of code that checks the reasonableness of some data produced by the program; for example, if the program carried out foreign exchange calculations then it might check that the dollar/pound rate was within sensible limits. If an assertion discovers data that is invalid, then an error has occurred, which is signalled to the test performance evaluator. The number of signals, which represents the number of errors discovered, is then used as a measure of test effectiveness.

The mechanism whereby new test data is generated, and which attempts to optimize test effectiveness, is not new. It relies on a branch of mathematics known as numerical optimization: the study of programming computers in order to find a maximum or minimum solution to a problem. Such techniques are used in discovering the optimal mix of solutions in a chemical reaction.

Adaptive testing, although intellectually appealing, has not been a so great a success as those techniques that rely on a knowledge of a program graph. My suspicion is that it is over-reliant on a technique for optimization which works well enough on numerical problems, such as finding the optimal dimensions of an aircraft's wing, but is too unsubtle for complex entities such as programs. In all the areas of software engineering with which I am familiar, it cries out for a researcher to apply the expert system technology that I described in Chapter 6.

The techniques I have described for automatically generating test data suffer from one major problem: they are computer-intensive. Take, for example, the graph-based systems that have been developed have to analyse a program, extract the program graph, discover which paths need to be executed, extract the set of equations, and then solve them. All these activities are highly resource-intensive, none more so than the solution of the equations. Many programs, indeed the vast majority, give rise to sets of equations so mathematically ugly that it can take hours for the computer to solve them. Not only are existing automatic testing systems inefficient, their development also consumes a large amount of resource and, in America in particular, a large amount of the time of testing academics was spent in writing modules for such systems.

Considering the amount of resource that was spent in the 1970s in adding to knowledge about automatic testing, it is no wonder that the results of two little-known American researchers shocked the testing community in the early 1980s. Joe Duran and Simeon Ntafos, two professors from the University of Texas, unveiled some startling results about testing at an international conference on software engineering held in San Diego.[3] The vast majority of the papers published in this series of proceedings are unremarkable, and merely report on relatively small gains in software engineering: a new design system may be announced, a new way of using mathematics for specification might be described, or industrial experiences with a novel software development technique related. No academic paper that has produced major change has appeared in the conference proceedings, apart from Ntafos and Duran's paper, which had the innocuous title of 'A report on random testing'.

What they had done was to take a number of programs and bombard them with random data: not data calculated by laboriously solving a set of equations, or data derived by using optimization, but random data. They used a simple piece of software that just selected test data from out of thin air. They discovered that, for many programs, such test data provided an excellent coverage: that it executed many of the paths in a program and also discovered a large number of subtle errors. Moreover, they demonstrated that one of the desirable properties of such random data was that the results from the tests using it could be used to predict the error rates of the software. Without a doubt these researchers, who had explored the simplest of all possible hypotheses about automatic test data selection, had virtually demolished much of the work that had preceded them.

This, then, is the history of automatic test data selection: a period of intense work in the 1970s, the publication of the Duran and Ntafos paper, and then relative quiet during the 1980s. This relative quiet was caused by a number of factors. First, it proved difficult to apply program graph methods to newer languages such as Ada, Prolog, and Pascal. Second, in the 1980s the problematic areas of specification and design had been identified, and testing, often associated with programming, became unfashionable. Third, Duran and Ntafos had demonstrated the futility of much of the automatic testing work that had been carried out. Fourth, industry had begun to discover some simple techniques for spotting errors in programs.

Probably the most effective, and simplest, technique for discovering errors was devised by two software engineers, Mike Fagan and Rodney Larson, who worked for IBM during the 1970s. They had discovered that the most effective way to discover errors in a software product was to ask someone else to look at it.

I can remember when I carried out research for my Ph.D., one of the tasks I had to carry out was to construct and correct a large, complicated software system. I would pour over the listings of my program for days on end, only for a colleague or a programmer at my computer centre, who was relatively unfamiliar with my work to lean over my shoulders and spot an error in seconds. The combination of being intimately involved in a programming problem, together with a subconscious desire not to find errors in one's own work, seem to act as a powerful break on the human error-detection mechanism.

All Fagan and Larson did was to formalize the process of others discovering your errors. They advocated the use of inspection teams, lead by a moderator, who would work through a program or a module, examine its logic, and check that it met its specification. The only aid that they used was a checklist of common errors and good practice that had been built up over a number of projects. Inspections at IBM were a major success. The only failures occurred when members of staff who were inspectors tried to settle old scores with ex-colleagues by an excessive zeal in criticizing their software. The inspection process became such a success that Fagan was awarded one of the highest bonuses ever given by IBM.[4] Such inspections now feature prominently on virtually every large project.

The inspection process can be supplemented with one of the strangest techniques used on software projects for discovering defects. It involves the deliberate introduction of errors in a program. A software project manager often wants to know how efficient his inspection teams are. A technique known as bebugging relies on the manager inserting artificial errors in the software before the inspections starts and examining how many of the errors the inspection team have discovered. This operation can be compared to the rather artificial solution to the problem of discovering how many fish there are in a pond:

> I have a pond which contains red fish. One day I wanted to discover how many fish there were in the pond. What I did was to call on my neighbour Joe who had a pond containing white fish. I asked Joe for a hundred of his fish, and poured them into my pond. The next day I went fishing in my pond. I caught 50 red fish and 25 white fish. From this result I concluded that there were two hundred fish in my pond.

The manager carries out the same process. He adds a specified number of errors, sets his inspection team to work, and checks how many of the artificial errors have been discovered. From this figure, the manager calculates the number of real errors using the same mathematics as the mythical fisherman. Not only is this technique an effective way of monitoring the efficiency of a key software process, it also puts the fear of hell into the inspection team and raises their productivity. I have a friend who is a quality assurance manager for a large company. One day he announced, out of the blue, that he was about to introduce bebugging as an evaluation technique. Within the month the average number of errors discovered by the inspection teams rose by over 50%, even though he had no resource, or any intention, to implement bebugging.

Another effective technique for judging test efficiency that involves the introduction of artificial errors is mutation testing.[5] It is a technique that overcomes the blindness that staff have about errors in the software that they develop. It is most useful just before acceptance testing, although it can be employed at any time after program code has been produced. Just before acceptance testing most managers feel confident that the tests that they have devised are adequate. However, they often yearn for some degree of confirmation. Mutation testing gives them that confidence. What this form of testing involves is the introduction of a series of small bugs into a program creating a series of programs each of which contain one error. Each program that has been modified in this way is known as a *mutant*.

Once a large number of mutants have been developed, they are tested using the data that is to be employed in acceptance testing. If the tests using the data discover the errors, then the mutant is said to have died. If the test data succeeds in killing off all the mutants then the data was adequate. However, if some mutants still live then the tester is in trouble: his test data has failed to discover a number of artificially inserted errors. He then has the task of inventing new test data that kills the mutants off.

Mutation testing is quite a computer-intensive technique. It is possible to produce a large number of mutants that, when tested, will use up large amounts of computer time. However, the technique is pretty effective when limited classes of mutants are generated. Mutation testing has the major advantage that it requires very little software support: merely a program that inserts the artificial errors. It also has a number of less-praiseworthy uses.

I know of one academic who uses little-known programming languages in his work. They are so little-known that no other users in his university employs them. Consequently, the staff of his computer centre are often threatening to retire the languages. However, towards the end of those months in which the threats are the most insistent, he runs a mutation testing system that generates thousands of programs in the languages. Consequently, when the language usage statistics are calculated his little-known languages come out top in terms of popularity.

One common solution to the problem of the emotional attachment of staff to their software is to set up an independent quality assurance department, that is completely separate from all projects. Its brief is to ensure that a system meets customer requirements. Its effectiveness lies in the fact that quality assurance departments are completely unconnected with a project, and that usually have a separate reporting line to the senior management of a company. Consequently, there are no emotional or political pressures to pass software as suitable for use.

Unfortunately, even independent quality assurance seems to be only a partial solution to the problem of errors. This is because it requires a special type of mentality to discover errors. The staff who are assigned to a quality assurance department have normally progressed into their position via software projects, where the prevailing ethos is that of delivery on time and to budget, with error detection coming a relatively poor third.

The failure of independent quality assurance has lead a number of American companies to set up organizations known as adversary teams. These teams are modelled on the black teams that were once a feature of some of the divisions of IBM. A black team is a collection of misfits and loners who would not normally find a place in a software project. They lack any creative impulse at all and find pleasure in destruction. The typical black team in an American software developer might contain a high-school drop-out,whose only interest in life apart from work is driving in demolition derbys; a high flying Ph.D. graduate who spends most of his salary on appointments with his analyst; a reformed ex-hacker; and an extremely competent software developer who once received poor treatment from a project manager and now has has the sole aim of gaining revenge on all project managers.

The only function of a black team is to devise ways of making a software system crash. Their skills are such that they can think of the most unlikely combinations of events that do this. They use a different vocabulary from normal development teams. A test succeeds if it crashes a system. It succeeds particularly well if it manages to produce some spectacular result, for example, locking out a whole system to users, or putting a system into an endless loop that can only be terminated by the time-consuming process of switching the computer off and re-initializing the system. The latter effect is one that all black teams aim for, particularly if there are other applications working on the computer affected.

The black teams are a particularly extreme example of antagonistic approaches to system testing. A slightly more acceptable version of the same philosophy is the bug bounty hunter. One of the most recent phenomena of the American software scene is the independent test company, many of which have emerged in San Francisco and New York. For a fee you pay such a company to send in representatives who will carry out the same process that the black teams carry out. However, there is a major difference between them and the black teams. The black teams were motivated by malice and a general grudge against the world: the bug bounty hunters are motivated by financial concerns. The normal form of contract with an independent test company is a flat fee, plus a bounty payment for each bug discovered.

Black teams have become successful because of the nature of their members. However, they have become more effective because of the increased sophistication of software tools available. A black team or bounty hunter uses such a tool to discover those parts of a system that are not executed by the developer's test data. They then devise tests that execute these areas. Almost invariably this discovers many serious errors. The use of black teams and bounty hunters is still in its infancy. However, they offer both an effective approach to software testing and a place on software projects for staff who would normally be expressing their destructive skills to the detriment of society.

Testing is regarded as one of the key activities in a software project. Thus, it is surprising that very little advance has been made in easing the testing process. The only major advance is the demonstration that automatic test data selection, via random generation of data, is a feasible technique. However, this is currently little used on projects.

Hardly any research work has been carried out on automating the processes of system testing and acceptance testing. The reason for this is that the data generated for these tests is produced by reading system specifications written in natural language, and even the staunchest supporters of artificial intelligence techniques would not claim that their subject will provide the tools for the analysis of such texts.

In many ways, all the advances possible in software testing have been made. Almost all these have been in the area of managerial techniques that ensure that quality assurance is progressed in a sensible way in a company. My suspicion is that the only gap left in commercial software testing involves a minor technology transfer problem concerning tools.

An impressive number of testing tools have been developed over the past decade. Probably, the best known is the profiler, which inserts software probes into a program under test. Whenever part of the program is executed, the software probe associated with that part writes information to a test data base that just says that it has been executed. When the program has completed execution, the test data base is printed out, and summary reports are produced that specify those parts of the program that have not been executed by test data. This provides information that enables the tester to develop further test data that covers the unaffected parts of the program under test.

Another useful tool that is now available for a number of programming languages is a static analyser. This examines the text of a program and discovers a number of errors that would be extremely difficult to discover during the actual running of a program. For example, a common error that is often committed is to define a storage area in the computer and forget to put data in it; it is this type of error that static analysers are excellent at detecting.

Another useful tool is the test harness. One of the time-consuming activities that a programmer has to carry out is that of writing a mini-program into which a program unit is to be fitted during unit testing. This mini-program sets up test files, sends the test data to the unit, and prints out the results from the test. The development of these mini-programs is repetitive and a number of software tools, known as test harnesses, have been developed that enable such a testing environment to be set up automatically, with little intervention from the tester.

Other test tools include test data library managers that carry out the mundane task of organizing a large library of files containing test data; software tools that simulate the action of an outside provider of data, such as a chemical reactor; and comparators that examine the massive amount of test results that have been generated, and compare them with the expected results that have been calculated by the tester.

Unfortunately, there is still limited use of many testing tools on current software projects. My prediction is that, in the first few years of the 1990s, if you visit a state-of-the-art software project you will find marginally tighter managerial quality assurance controls, together with a much increased use of these tools.

# References

1.    See, for example, a system developed at the University of Massachusetts, described by its author, Lori Clarke, in the paper: A System to Generate Test Data

and Symbolically Execute Programs, L. Clarke, *IEEE Transactions on Software Engineering*, **2**, 3. 1976.

2.   A good description of adaptive testing can be found in the paper: An Automated Program Testing Methodology and its Implementation, D. M. Andrews and J. P Benson, *Proceedings 5th International Conference on Software Engineering*. 1981.

3.   A Report on Random Testing, J. W. Duran and S. Ntafos, *Proceedings 5th International Conference on Software Engineering*. 1981.

4.   A good description of the inspection technique is contained in the paper written by Fagan: Design and Code Inspection to Reduce Errors in Program Development, M. Fagan, *IBM Systems Journal*, **15**, 3. 1976.

5.   Mutation Testing: Ideas, Examples, Problems and Prospects, T. Budd, In *Computer Program Testing*, B. Chandarasekaran and S. Radicchi (Eds.). Amsterdam: Elsevier-North Holland. 1981.

# 14

# Climbing the Tower of Babel

One of the features of the 1970s was the large number of arguments about programming languages. Whole conferences were organized during which the merits of Pascal, APL, FORTRAN, and COBOL, were debated at inordinate length. I can remember one particular debate that occurred in the academic institution that I worked in during the early 1970s. We had to decide on the programming language to be used to teach programming. The two choices were a little-known and convoluted language called Algol68, or the popular teaching language Pascal; the decision took a number of months. During this period friendships were strained and temporarily terminated, and meetings were held which were characterized by a quality of spleen that only academics are capable of generating.

The tragedy of the arguments of the 1970s was that they were essentially sterile: we did not recognize that programming was the easiest task that occurred in a software project. Current figures now put the amount of project resource devoted to it at between 5 and 10% of project cost. Furthermore, we now realize that activities such as design and specification are the most important, and can affect the success or otherwise of a software project. In the case of my own department's argument about Pascal *vis-a-vis* Algol68, I was on the losing side. However, if we had chosen the language that I supported it wouldn't have mattered one iota: we made it a tenet of our programming courses that we taught programming, not the detailed syntax of a programming language, so the choice was irrelevant.

Debate about programming languages still occurs. However, the nature of the arguments has changed and become more important. Previously the arguments concerned the pros and cons of similar languages. Although many computer practitioners regard languages such as COBOL and FORTRAN as different on the surface, they are essentially the same. They are procedural languages that have the same control structures, are based on conventional architectures and, operate on the same type of data.

Currently, the arguments which are being voiced, are about languages that are radically different, and that are based on widely differing computational models. These arguments are more important in that they have a major bearing on the activities of design and specification. Hence we can no longer regard debate about programming languages as sterile.

The next ten years will see four main categories of programming language competing for use. They are procedural languages, logic languages, functional languages, and object-oriented languages. Since procedural languages have been used since the beginning of computing it is only fitting that I deal with them first.

I have reproduced a small program written in a procedural language below. The language only exists in my imagination: current procedural programming languages are so complex on the surface that their complexity would get in the way of the points I want to make.

> Set *Sum* to 0
> REPEAT
>> Input a *number*
>> Add it to *Sum*
> 3 TIMES
> Print out *Sum*

The program above consists of a series of instructions that are to be obeyed by a computer, and that access two locations in the computer's memory called Sum and number. Before the program is run these locations will be empty; they will look like:

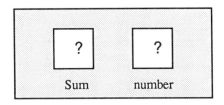

The question marks stands for the fact that the contents are not known. When the program above is run, the computer steps through the program, line by line, placing data in a memory location, or overwriting a memory location. The line 'Set *Sum* to 0', places a value zero in the memory location *Sum*. The computer's memory will now look like:

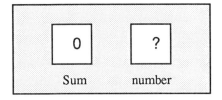

The computer will next obey the lines 'Input a *number*' and 'Add it to *Sum*' three times. The lines 'REPEAT' and '3 TIMES' are known as a loop. The function of a loop is to instruct the computer to obey a series of instructions a number of times; in the case of the program above, the loop instructs the computer to obey the instructions 'Input a *number*' and 'Add it to *Sum*' three times.

The first time the loop is obeyed, the instruction 'Input a *number*' is encountered, and has to be obeyed. What happens is that the user of the program sees on the screen of his computer a character that invites him to type in a number. Usually this character is a question mark or the > character. The user then types in the number, and it is placed in the location *number* by the computer. If the user types in the number 23 then the computer's memory now looks like:

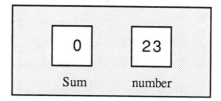

The next instruction that the computer has to obey is 'Add it to *Sum*' This means that the contents of the number location has to be added to the contents of the *Sum* location. Since there was only a zero in *Sum* the computer's memory now looks like:

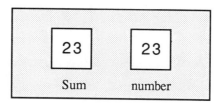

The loop has now been obeyed once. Since the computer has been instructed to obey the loop three times, another two passes are required. On the second pass the computer again encounters the instruction 'Input a *number*' If the user types in the number 19 then the contents of the computer's memory now becomes:

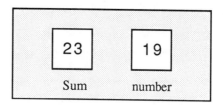

The next instruction to be encountered is 'Add it to *Sum*' This results in 19 being added to the contents of *Sum*, the computer's memory then becomes:

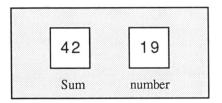

One more pass through the loop is now required. If the user types in 12 then the memory will take on the values shown in the two snapshots shown below:

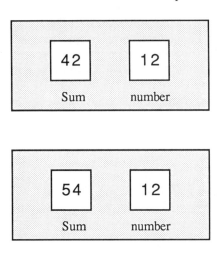

The first snapshot shows the values after the user has typed in 12, the second snapshot shows the values after the instruction 'Add it to *Sum*' has been obeyed. The loop has been obeyed three times. The only instruction remaining to be obeyed is 'Print out *Sum*'. What this instruction does is to take the number stored in *Sum* (54) and display it on the screen of the computer that has just run the program.

The effect of the program is to ask the user for three numbers (12, 19, 23), form the sum of these numbers (54), and then display the sum to the user. This is obviously a trivial program. However, it does illustrate the main concepts that underpin procedural programming languages: that these languages describe the movement of data about a computer system, from a user, via his keyboard, to the computer memory; then from the memory, back to the user, via his vdu screen. Procedural languages directly reflect the mechanics of the computer which they program. If it were possible to monitor the flow of data around a computer system, then you would see the behaviour that was exactly described by a program in a procedural language.

The majority of industrial software development is carried out using procedural languages. The language FORTRAN, which dates from the early 1950s, is used for numerical applications such as simulating chemical reactions;

COBOL is a procedural language used for commercial-data processing applications, such as those found in banking, accounting, and insurance; Pascal and BASIC are used for teaching programming, and are also used in some industrial projects; PL/1 is a language developed by IBM that was intended to be used in both numerical and commercial data-processing applications.

Although, on the surface many procedural programming languages look different, they are still the same underneath. They still conform to the processing model that I have described above. This model is based on a computer architecture known as the Von-Neumann architecture, named after John von Neumann, the inventor of the concept of a program. Each procedural language that has been developed, and there have been myriads, still describes the passage of data to and from a user, to and from memory, via a processor.

The history of procedural languages is essentially one of a major breakthrough: the invention of FORTRAN in the late 1950s, followed by the gradual improvement of an existing language, either through the invention of new languages for other application areas, or via the incorporation of better facilities in existing languages. For example, the development of COBOL is an instance of a new language being designed for a different application area from FORTRAN, while the development of new dialects of BASIC, incorporating changes in attitude to programming, is an example of a less dramatic advance.

What many see as the final stage in the development of procedural languages was the invention of the language Ada. This is a programming language intended for real-time embedded applications. These are applications in which a microcomputer is embedded into an existing electronic system, and in which there they may be stringent response-time requirements. A typical application for Ada is a ship-borne defence system, where the computer forms an integral part of a complicated system of radars, missiles, heavy machine guns, and decoy launchers.

Such a system has a very stringent response time: missiles must be launched, guns aimed, and aluminium decoy material ejected into the air, within seconds of a potential aggressor being spotted by radar. Many of the operations that such a system has to carry out are mechanical and would, themselves, occupy some seconds of time; hence there is often a requirement on the computer in a ship-borne defence system to respond in milliseconds.

The development history of Ada is unique. In the late 1970s the American Department of Defense, the largest buyer of software in the world, started becoming very worried about the large amount of software that it found itself maintaining. They discovered that they had a major problem: much of the software was written in bewildering variety of programming languages; it was perceived by planners that if nothing was done, there would be little resources left in the 1980s for new software development. All the resources planned for would be used on retraining programmers in a new programming language, allowing them time to become familiar with a language, and on the maintenance process itself, which, for many systems, would be a major headache as they often consisted of sub-systems that were programmed in different languages.

The solution adopted by the Department of Defense was standardization. They decided that from a certain date in the 1980s all new software would be developed using a common language. This language was called Ada, after Ada, Countess Lovelace, who, in the early nineteenth century, programmed the first computer: Charles Babbage's analytical engine.

What was unique about the development of Ada was that its design was put out to competitive tender. Four possible designs were selected and the winner was announced in 1979. What surprised many commentators was that the winning language was European in origin. It was developed by a collection of French, American, British and West German language experts associated with the computer manufacturer Honeywell-Bull. The major input into the design came from Europe. This is quite clear from looking at Ada, which bears little resemblance to the major American programming languages COBOL, FORTRAN, and PL/1, but which looks like the offspring of the European programming language Pascal.

Ada is a very big language. It contains virtually every improvement in language design that has occurred in the last two decades. It contains excellent facilities for controlling tasks that can occur concurrently; it has an extensive range of facilities for storing and accessing data; and, furthermore, it enables the developer to produce software that can be reused time and time again.[1] Although many languages enable software reuse to take place, Ada contains the most comprehensive set of facilities for reuse that have been designed into a programming language. The strengths of Ada also cause some of its weaknesses. Since the designers of the language took advantage of all the advances in programming during the 1960s and 1970s the language is big, in fact it is very big. A number of commentators claim that Ada has become such a Baroque monstrosity that it represents the logical end of procedural programming language design.

Ada is certainly a very complicated language, and requires a massive training investment from companies who wish to use it. Nevertheless, because it is mandatory on American defence projects, and will soon be mandatory on British defence projects, it will be a major language in the 1980s and the 1990s.

The other major procedural language development over the last decade has been the fourth-generation language. In Chapter 2 I briefly described some of the dangers of using these languages. In this chapter I shall try and redress the balance. A feature of 1970s computing was the increasing use of databases. The word 'database' has a very specialized meaning in computing, although almost everybody who has a store of data tends to use the word. The word 'database', properly used, means a large store of data held on a computer, where the relationships between individual items are also stored. For example, databases are used in airline seat reservation systems where details of planes, passengers, flights, and airports are held in large, stored files. Also stored in these files are

CLIMBING THE TOWER OF BABEL

the relationships between these objects; for example, the fact that a flight departs from particular airport, or the fact that a particular passenger is travelling on a particular flight, would be stored.

There was a massive growth in the use of database technology in the 1970s. The reason was that applications were becoming so complex and large, with so many relations between the objects being stored, that specialized database systems were the only way to process the data.

A major feature of these database systems was query languages. These were languages that could be used by naive users to retrieve data. For example, a query language would be employed by a booking clerk to find out seat availability in an airline reservation system. In the early 1970s these languages were fairly primitive. The user typed in a simple set of words and the computer responded. For example, in an airline booking system, the clerk might type in the words:

PASSENGER LIST BA102

This would then display all the passengers on flight BA102. Early query languages were a major success: they were simple and they allowed naive users such as bank clerks, account clerks, and businessmen to retrieve information in a matter of seconds; certainly in a much shorter time than the hard-pressed computing department could manage.

However, during the 1970s, with the advent of the microcomputer, applications became much more complicated and query languages followed this trend. For example, the users of airline reservation systems often needed to make complicated queries about long flight plans that involved a number of airlines. In response to this increase in complexity, query languages became bigger and more complicated.

Fourth-generation languages are a descendant of these early query languages. However, they have become distinct entities in themselves, and offer many more facilities. A typical fourth-generation language contains query facilities, programming facilities, programs to set up databases and to display complex graphical charts, together with programs that enable the user to carry out what if processing. In this form of processing a user queries a database by asking questions such as: 'What if I order a large amount of stock next month: will we sell it all?' or What if we add another flight to the Rome route: will we make an increased profit?' Many fourth-generation languages also offer sophisticated mathematical and financial facilities; these enable the user to make business decisions on the basis of past data such as sales figures or stock depletion figures.

I have already described some of the dangers of fourth-generation languages in Chapter 2. The positive thing to say about them is that they offer developers who wish to carry out prototyping an extremely powerful tool-kit. Unfortunately, the opportunities for using fourth-generation languages are limited. They are only intended for commercial-data processing applications such as those found in banking and retailing. Many of these applications are so well known, with a wealth of experience from both developers and customers, that prototyping is not really required.

In Chapter 8 I described how functional languages, also known as fifth-generation languages, have been developed to overcome major problems that are being being encountered with conventional hardware architectures. Another feature of functional languages is their elegance. The word 'elegance' is difficult to explain when used to describe a programming language, indeed it is difficult to understand what it means when used in day-to-day discourse. The best explanation is that a programming language is elegant when its programs are succinct, but not so terse that other programmers have difficulty in understanding them, a big advantage in these days when program maintenance can occupy as much as 70% of project resource.

Procedural languages are pretty inelegant. For example, a simple program in COBOL to process and print a file can occupy over thirty lines of text. Functional languages are elegant as they do not concern themselves with the detailed step-by-step processing that procedural languages are required to do.

An example of a program written in functional language is shown below. The language is HOPE, which has been developed at Edinburgh University and Imperial College, London.

```
average(l) <= sum(l) div count(l)
sum(nil) <= 0
sum(n::l) <= n+sum(l)
count(nil) <=0
count(n::l) <= 1+count(l)
```

The first line is straightforward. It states that the average of a list of numbers $l$ is equal to the sum of the numbers in $l$, divided by the count of the numbers in $l$. The symbols <= stand for the words: 'is equal to'. The next two lines define *sum*. The second line states that the sum of the empty list of numbers (nil) is zero. The third line states that the sum of a list containing a number $n$, followed by a list $l$, is equal to $n$ plus the sum of the numbers in $l$. The fourth and fifth lines define what is meant by *count*. The fourth line states that the count of the number of elements in an empty list (nil) is zero. The fifth line states that the count of the elements in a list consisting of a number $n$, followed by a list $l$ of numbers, is equal to 1 plus the count of the elements in $l$.

Functional languages, such as HOPE, seem to have a bright future once they can be interfaced with modern computer architectures. However, there is one factor which that probably limit their growth. Programming in a functional language is totally unlike any programming that is carried out today. Procedural languages involve the programmer thinking in terms of the detailed movement of data in a computer system. This view of a program, which is close to what happens in a computer, is taught in our schools, and the vast majority of our universities and polytechnics. Programming involving functional languages involves thinking more mathematically: in terms of equations. Since the vast majority of programmers have been totally immersed in a procedural culture there will be a massive training and education effort needed. Also, when functional languages become a commercial proposition, there will be a large amount of procedural software in existence. This software represents a major capital investment that, understandably, will not be retired by software developers, but will be maintained for many years. These two factors will mean that, at best, we can expect only a gradual adoption of functional languages by industry.

Another category of fifth-generation languages is those based on logic, of which the best-known example is PROLOG.[2] The history of logic programming is a strange one. The idea that mathematical logic can be used to program computers is not new. In 1971 an American computer scientist, Carl Hewitt, developed a programming language called PLANNER that contained the germ of many of the ideas embodied in logic programming languages. However, even the most ardent proponents of logic programming would admit that until 1981 logic programming existed only on the fringes of computer science.

This was changed in 1981 when the Japanese Ministry of International Trade and Industry announced the creation of a special laboratory, called the Institute for New Generation Technology (ICOT), which was intended to pursue the development of fifth-generation computing technology. A major component of the Japanese Programme was the use of the expert system technology that I described in Chapter 6. This came as quite a surprise to the international computing community, many of whom had never heard of expert systems. However, what was even a greater surprise was the adoption of the logic programming language PROLOG as the software medium for the project.

The reason for the surprise was that the majority of artificial intelligence applications that had been developed, including the vast majority of expert systems, had been implemented using the programming language LISP. This was an artificial intelligence programming language that had a long pedigree, a large amount of expertise, a not inconsiderable amount of teaching material, and a number of well-designed software environments.

I was puzzled by the Japanese approach to information technology. In the past Japan had affected the industries of the Western world, not by adopting radical practices, but by doing conventional things better. For example, in manufacturing, the Japanese industry's obsessive approach to quality assurance is streets ahead of the practices adopted in most Western industries but, nevertheless, is modelled on the practices that were imported into Japan by the Americans just after the Second World War.

A cynic would have good reason to think that the ICOT project was a gigantic attempt to blow Western information technology off-course, while Japan developed improved software systems and hardware architectures to the point where they were cheaper and better than existing Western products. Even though Japan had continually demonstrated that it was at its most dangerous when working with current technology, its proposed use of advanced technology galvanized a number of Western Governments into action. Here in Britain it lead to the establishment of the Alvey programme. This was a Government initiative aimed at improving the United Kingdom's competitive position in information technology and in which expert systems and logic programming figured very strongly.

A direct result of the Japanese intentions was a massive increase in interest in PROLOG. From being an interesting sideshow it established itself, virtually overnight, as a major programming language, with logic programming achieving a significance that very few of practitioners could have predicted. In Britain, which possessed the majority of the logic programming experience in the world, if offered us the opportunity, for once, of holding our heads high amongst major competitors.

Logic languages and logic programming are based on a model that is dissimilar to both those used in functional languages, and current conventional languages such as FORTRAN and COBOL. The central idea is that program execution consists of carrying out deductions, rather than fetching and manipulating data extracted from the main store of the computer. To illustrate this I have reproduced a simple PROLOG program below. It consists of a series of rules written one to a line:

```
ancestor(X,Y) <- parent (X,Y)
ancestor(X,Z) <- parent(X,Y),ancestor(Y,Z).
parent(arthur, william).
parent(william, david).
parent(david, ben).
parent(ben,robert).
```

The first rule states that for any two people $X$ and $Y$, if $Y$ is an ancestor of $X$ then one possibility is that $Y$ is the parent of $X$. The second rule states that for any two people $X$ and $Z$, if $Z$ is an ancestor of $X$ then there exists a person $Y$ who is the parent of $X$ and who has an ancestor $Z$. The next lines state that *William* is the parent of *Arthur*, *David* is the parent of *William* etc. When this program is executed, say to find all the ancestors of *Arthur*, then the computer deduces from these rules that *William, David, Ben*, and *Robert* are the ancestors.

Logic programming programming languages have a number of appealing features. First, in a similar way to functional languages, the structure of a logic programs is extremely simple. Second, logic programs correspond closely to the structure of expert systems; probably the most successful use of logic programming languages is in developing such systems. Third, it is possible to write complex programs very quickly in a logic programming language, this makes them a good medium for software prototyping. Fourth, PROLOG in particular, contains facilities that enable programmers to develop language processors easily. Such processors translate between a high-level language and the language of the computer. It enables the developer to design and implement new programming languages in a matter of weeks rather than years.

Unfortunately, there is one major stumbling block to logic programming. The only successful implementation of the idea is PROLOG. To write efficient programs in PROLOG the programmer has to include instructions that are not written in logic and, in fact, resemble the instructions in a procedural language. This makes programming in PROLOG a very difficult task indeed. These, so-called *extralogical* facilities, can lead to such incredibly subtle errors that even the most experienced programmer can take days tracking them down.

I learned PROLOG two years ago, in order to develop some software to help me in my research. In learning the language I experienced a phenomenon that I had never experienced before. During the initial learning stage I used only the logic programming facilities of the language. I could write programs that were elegant, readable, and free of errors; moreover, I could develop these programs very quickly. However, I soon realized that if I just used pure logic then the programs that I developed would be extremely slow. In order to develop more efficient programs I learned the extralogical facilities of the language, and experienced one of the most frustrating periods that I have spent learning about any software system. The change in learning difficulty was a large discrete step: it became extremely difficult to develop correct, readable programs. To make any headway I had to adopt a model of computation that was procedural in nature in order to understand what was actually happening inside the computer. This was a model which was completely at variance with the conceptual idea behind PROLOG.

It is always a bad sign to encounter a massive increase in difficulty in learning a language. Certainly, all the other languages that I had learned previously, including functional languages, had resulted in me traversing a smooth learning curve, which, although steeper than the initial learning curve of PROLOG, did not include a massive conceptual jump.

The proponents of logic programming will point out that PROLOG is an imperfect example of a logic programming language; that much more resource spent on research will eventually lead to languages in which procedural facilities will be absent. Unfortunately, at present, no researcher seems anywhere close to this large breakthrough. Nevertheless, PROLOG is still a useful language. If you are considering prototyping or developing an expert system, then it is a language you should, at least, consider seriously.

The other major strand in programming language design has been the emergence of object-oriented languages. To understand why such languages have been developed it would be useful to repeat briefly the description of the software development process that I presented in Chapter 1.

Conventional software development consists of an analyst taking a statement of requirements for a system from a customer, and producing a specification that describes what that system is to do. This specification is almost invariably couched in terms of the functions of the system. For example, the specification for a banking system would say that the system would display account information, issue cheque books, and construct customer statements. A designer takes this specification and then produces a design consisting of modules, sets of which implement each function identified during requirements analysis. These modules are then coded and implemented.

Unfortunately, this approach leads to problems during maintenance, when the functions of a system change in response to changing user requirements. Functions are often so intimately related to each other that a change in coding, which takes place in response to a change in a function, often requires changes to the program code of other functions.

Object-oriented development attempts to overcome this problem by carrying out requirements analysis in a different way. Instead of identifying functions, the analyst identifies the objects in a system, their properties, and the operations they undergo. For example, in an air-traffic control system, typical objects would be planes, radar installations, and operator consoles. Typical operations that these objects might take part in are the updating of a plane's position, the transmission of a radar signal, etc.

These objects, together with the operations that apply to them, are then packaged up into modules in a programming language. Experience so far has indicated that systems developed in this way are extremely easy to maintain. Any changes to a system usually just involve the introduction of new objects and operations or small changes to existing objects and operations.

To cope with object-oriented methods a number of new languages have been designed and are becoming easily available. Typical languages include Object-C, Smalltalk, Object-Pascal, and, most importantly, Ada.[3] All these languages contain facilities for defining objects and operations, and enable objects to be isolated from each other so that a change to an object, say during maintenance, does not affect any others.

It is always difficult to predict the future. However, some trends are quite clear. In commercial data processing, COBOL will still have a major part to play in software development for at least ten to twenty years. There is a massive amount of investment in existing systems written in conventional languages; this will not be written off over a short time. However, I would not be surprised to see versions of COBOL in the 1990s which incorporated object-oriented facilities.

For real-time applications another thing is clear: that Ada will become the major language. The very fact that both the United States Department of Defense, and our own Ministry of Defence, insist on its use, will ensure that it will be the real-time language for this century. However, it is difficult to predict the form that conventional languages will take after this. Ada feels like a language that represents the end of an era. Almost all the developments in programming theory over the last twenty years have been incorporated in the language and, apart from refinements to its object-oriented facilities, it is difficult to think of any further improvement that might be required.

The fascinating question is what is the future for functional languages, logic languages, and object-oriented languages. Both functional and logic languages are really waiting for the big breakthrough. The future use of functional languages depends on a breakthrough in research on implementing them on multi-processor computers In the early 1980s substantial work has started in this country and America to develop novel architectures. Such architectures initially involve the use of hundreds of processors and, eventually, tens of thousands of processors. Early simulation studies have shown that while it is not possible to achieve a linear increase of power with such computers, as processors are added, there is still a very large increase that could not be achieved by current architectures.

The future use of logic languages depends on a breakthrough in implementing logic in a form that is not encumbered by the kludgy, procedural facilities that disfigure PROLOG . In many ways this breakthrough seems a longer way off than the architecture breakthroughs required for functional languages

The most interesting question about future software development involves object-oriented languages. Systems developed using such languages have proved exceptionally clean and easy to maintain. Developers claim that thinking in terms of objects and operations is a more natural way of thinking about systems and, hence, will lead to a reduction in analysis and design costs. My feeling is that, since object-oriented languages are based on procedural ideas, during the interregnum when functional or logic languages are being improved any growth in programming technology will manifest itself in new object-oriented languages, or in object-oriented additions to existing languages.

One of the heartening features of recent development in programming languages is the movement away from issues involving minor modifications to the existing features of procedural languages, towards two bigger concerns. The first concern is that of simplicity and elegance. Procedural programming languages are becoming baroque monstrosities, and any movement away from this should be welcomed. The second concern is that is that programming is no longer the major task in software projects and that programming languages should reflect this. Languages such as Ada now have major facilities for design; functional languages and logic languages are an excellent medium for prototyping during requirements analysis; and programs in functional languages represent a mathematical specification of a system. It is because of the fact that developers and researchers have taken notice of these concerns, that programming language design, once a moribund research area, has again achieved a major importance in computer science.

# References

1. An excellent text book that describes the Ada language and how to develop big systems in Ada is: *Software Engineering with Ada*, G. Booch, Menlo Park, Calif: Benjamin Cummings. 1987.

2. It is extremely difficult to write a good introductory textbook on PROLOG. Probably the best that has been written is: *PROLOG: A Relational Language and its Applications*, J. Malpas, Englewood Cliffs, N.J.: Prentice-Hall. 1987.

3. A special issue of *Byte* magazine is devoted to object-oriented languages. Many of the articles in this issue are very readable. The issue is Volume 11, No. 8, August 1986.

# 15

# Artificial intelligence in finance

In Chapter 6 I described a branch of artificial intelligence concerned with the development of expert systems: computer programs that encapsulate knowledge from a human expert and that, theoretically anyway, eventually replace that expert. In the same chapter I described the way in which industry experts predicted that expert systems would work in the future.

When the Japanese made their announcement about the role of artificial intelligence in their future systems, the reaction of Western scientists was one of disbelief. What was being proposed was a complete break from conventional software development. Moreover, it was a break that seemed to have little going for it: when the Japanese announced their plans you could count the number of successful expert systems on one hand, and the number of researchers familiar with this technology was probably no more than twenty. With hindsight the move into such a limited area can seen to be a wise one: it makes good economic sense to target an area with little intellectual competition.

The West's response to the Japanese plans was immediate. Governmental research and development projects were rapidly put together: Great Britain announced the Alvey project, the EEC the massive Esprit project, while the United States government sponsored a large number of individual projects through their existing funding agencies.

We have now reached the stage where there is a sizeable expert system community. It is only now, five years after the ballyhoo, that an objective assessment of the penetration of expert systems be made. Recently, I wrote a report on the impact of artificial intelligence on finance and business.[1] One of the remarkable things that I discovered was that although it is still early days when it comes to the volume of expert system technology being employed in the financial field, there is a great variety in the way the technology is being used. Furthermore, the most successful applications of artificial intelligence technology, certainly in business and finance, seem to deviate quite markedly from the ideals of the Japanese.

Probably one of the most impressive examples of artificial intelligence technology being used in the field, and probably the use furthest away from that which the Japanese envisaged, was carried out by analysts from the accountants Arthur Anderson & Co.[2] They used some artificial intelligence tools for prototyping, producing an early version of a software system that could be shown to a customer and discussed before real software development commenced.

Prototyping is now becoming a popular activity for software developers who have to cope with large numbers of fuzzy requirements from their customers. It enables an inefficient working system to be demonstrated early on in a software project. Prototyping is a distinct improvement on the large amorphous requirements documents that often form the basis of discussions between the developer and the customer about what a proposed system is to do..

The Chicago office of Arthur Anderson was charged with developing a system for accounting for the movement of equipment from one oil lease to another. Although this sounds a relatively straightforward task their analysts soon discovered that massive complexities arose because of the fact that a lot of the material objects that were moved around were co-owned. Because of this, and because the new system was doing much more than automating a well-understood manual system, the analysts tried prototyping. They turned to an unusual tool (for prototyping that is): the expert system shell. An expert system shell is a software system that allows a developer to produce an expert system very quickly.

The team at Arthur Anderson adopted a six-step approach to development. The first step was for an accounting expert from one of the oil companies involved to discuss the application with the team. From this discussion ten specific material movement cases were identified, and the results in terms of their effect on the systems accounting database were discovered. The second step was to develop a system that processed these ten cases successfully. This took less than a week. The third step was further case analysis. Here unusual cases were analysed, or cases for which no historical paperwork resulted. The fourth stage was a process of knowledge refinement: more and more cases were added, until all thirty-five possible cases for the application were incorporated into the prototype. This took five weeks. The fifth step was user sign-off. A one-page report was produced from the shell which showed the characteristics of all the cases and the results in terms of changes in the contents of the accounting database. This was shown to oil company experts and signed off as being correct. The final stage was documentation of the system. It involved the analysts translating the cases to a standard requirements specification notation. The model developed from the expert system shell also generated a full set of test data, which was then used to test a conventionally developed system.

An application nearer to what was originally envisaged as an expert system has recently been developed at the University of Southern Carolina for corporate analysis of the petroleum wholesale industry.[3] It is based on the concept of the intelligent spreadsheet. This system: FINEX, which is currently used by a number of wholesalers, analyses the strengths and weaknesses of a company by looking at specific ratios of numeric data found in its annual financial statement. Typical ratios that are used by FINEX are total asset turnover, profit margin, and accounts receivable turnover.

A company's financial statement is build up using a conventional spreadsheet, the ratios are calculated, and the resulting data is then transferred to an expert system that acts in two modes: interpretative mode and analysis mode. Interpretative mode uses the ratios calculated by the spreadsheet to carry out an analysis of the company's financial state. To do this it employs a model developed by the DuPont Corporation that uses the financial figures found in the company's balance sheet to calculate a measure of its health. The interpretative mode of working has very little to do with expert systems: the same type of calculation could be carried out by a conventional computer program. What makes the FINEX system different is the second mode of working: analysis mode.

Analysis mode uses information that is not contained in the spreadsheet. For example, if the spreadsheet had calculated that a company's gross margin is low, then it would ask a series of questions whose answers could only be supplied by the financial or marketing staff of the company. Typical questions would be:

- Is your competition stiff?
- Does the stiff competition require you to lower prices?
- Is your inventory turnover low?
- Have the prices charged to you by your suppliers risen within the last year?

From these questions, and others, FINEX might reach the conclusion that competition has caused the company to offer more lenient credit terms, raising its accounts-receivable level and thereby lowering its gross margin.

Financial ratios are proving a popular analysis medium for expert systems in America. Arthur Anderson have developed a much deeper expert system for the analysis of financial statements. It is based on work carried out by Marinus Bouwman, an American academic whose research is concerned with the process of how decision makers, particularly those in the financial industry, make decisions.[4]

Arthur Anderson was hired by the Securities and Exchange Commission to explore the feasibility of an automated system that could monitor financial filings for compliance with American Securities laws, and also convert the data submitted to the SEC into an easily accessible form.[5]

The system that the team at Arthur Anderson developed processed a company's financial documents, including statements and notes to the accounts. Two knowledge bases support the system: one contains accounting and financial information and the other contains knowledge that is used when processing notes to the accounts. The system is more sophisticated than FINEX and, consequently, requires a very powerful artificial intelligence workstation. Currently, it represents the peak of achievement of expert systems applications in accounting.

Recent pioneering work on expert system aid for tax applications has been carried out at the University of Manchester Institute of Science and

Technology.[6] Researchers there have developed an expert system that advises on the apportionment of income of certain companies, called close companies, amongst the companies' shareholders. It guards against wealthy shareholders, who pay tax at higher rates, deciding not to pay dividends from the companies that they control, in order to save on their tax bill.

The current provisions governing close companies can be found in Schedule 16 of the 1972 Finance Act. This act gives the Inland Revenue the power to apportion the income of close companies to the companies' shareholders. It is an area of legislation that gives the Inland Revenue major problems. Tax inspectors in the past have had to use extremely lengthy manuals to make their decisions. Since there is a shortage of tax inspectors in this area, inspectors who are inexperienced in close company law have to deal with a large number of cases. Using a manual this can take a number of hours. An expert system was developed that enabled this time to be cut down.

The system was developed on an ICL 2900 mainframe using an expert system shell known as ICL ADVISER. The knowledge base was built up by referencing three sources of information: statutes, Inland Revenue training notes, and the tax inspectors' reference manual. Little contact was made with tax experts since these sources of information were very comprehensive.

These, then, are some of the systems that I examined when writing a recent report on artificial intelligence applications in business and finance. They are typical of a general trend in the utilization of expert systems. A trend that is completely different from the one that industry experts predicted in the early 1980s: one of large systems, with complex knowledge databases, completely replacing the human expert. The actual use of these systems in finance and business is quite different and falls into two areas.

The first is the use of artificial intelligence languages and development systems for prototyping. One of the major expansion areas in software development is prototyping. By building a quick and dirty version of a software system, early in the software project, developers are finding that the error-strewn task of finding out what a customer requires can be considerably eased. A number of developers are discovering that the best way of constructing a quick and dirty version of a system is to use artificial intelligence technology: either expert system shells or artificial intelligence programming languages. Moreover, they are beginning to find that such prototypes can be changed very easily to react to external events such as mergers, acquisitions, and changes in legislation.

One of the common claims that I came across when carrying out my survey is that, since the knowledge base of an expert system contains sets of rules expressed in a quasi-natural-language form, the process of modifying the system in response to change can be trivial, often involving a small number of modifications to a few rules. With conventional software systems, which contain large amounts of program code, change is a more resource-intensive and error-prone activity, often involving software staff tracking through reams and reams of program print-out. Both the equipment movement and tax system described earlier are excellent examples of the power of artificial intelligence technology as a development medium for systems that can be prototyped and then modified when change occurs.

The second way that expert systems use differs from that which was predicted in the early 1980s is in the way that they are employed. The vast majority of expert systems used for financial applications tend to be decision-support systems. Instead of taking over the functions of staff such as financial analysts, expert systems are being used to carry out a large amount of pre-processing, and to implement functions such as spotting anomalies in data or drawing attention to figures that have given trouble in the past. Both the financial ratio systems described earlier fall into this category.

The early 1990s will prove a watershed for artificial intelligence technology. Progress in developing large expert systems, that can completely replace the human expert has proved exceptionally slow. It seems that once an expert system gets to a particular size, complexity problems set in, resulting in long development times and also, once they are installed, poor response times for the user. However, expert systems used as decision aids could be a major growth area.

There are a number of factors that will ensure a rapid growth of decision support systems in the financial industry: financial markets are becoming more volatile and moving faster, consequently, there is less time for decision making; the global financial network provides a decision maker with much more choices in term of investment strategy than even compared with five years ago; with the advent of computerized trading much more financial information is available; the current shake-out in financial services in this country has increased competition, this means that financial decision makers have to make more and more optimal decisions; finally, the consequences of incorrect decisions are becoming more serious: picking a poor time to sell equities can make a difference of hundreds of thousands of pounds to a portfolio manager

These factors, together with the bad press that current automatic programmed trading systems have attracted, should lead to an explosion in decision-support systems. In America, at least, the expert system seems to be one of the main conduits for this explosion, being used in a way that its original proponents never really envisaged.

If the growth in the use of expert systems continues in an application area where all the conditions are right for automated decision support, then the ballyhoo of the 1980s will at least be partially vindicated; if not, then we may have to conclude that the excitement about expert systems was really just the result of the hype that artificial intelligence has attracted during the last two decades.

# References

1.  *Artificial Intelligence in Business and Finance.* Information Technology Briefings. Available from the author.

2.  Six Steps to AI-based Functional Prototyping, R. Weisman, *Datamation*, 33, August. 1987.

3.  FINEX: An Expert System for Financial Analysis, L. Kerschberg and L. Dickinson, *Proceedings 5th International Workshop on Expert Systems and their Application*, Agence de l'Informatique, Paris la Defense, France. 1985.

4.  Human Diagnostic Reasoning by Computer: An Illustration from Financial Analysis, M. J. Bouwman, *Management Science*, **29**, 6. 1983.

5.  FSA: Applying AI Techniques to the Familiarisation Phase of Financial Decision Making, C. Mui and W. E. McCarthy, *IEE Expert*, Fall. 1987.

6.  The Development of an Expert Tax System. A. E. Roycroft, and P. Loucopoulos, *Proceedings 5th International Workshop on Expert Systems and their Application*, Agence de l'Informatique, Paris la Defense, France. 1985.

# 16

# Dragons, dungeons, and software documentation

Every software project uses documentation. If you walk into the offices of any project team you will find reams and reams of paper that describe the state of the project. There will be documents that describe the software: functional specifications, system designs, and print-outs of program code. There will also be documents that describe project progress; for example, project plans, reports from senior project staff, accounts of meeting, and test reports. The problem with this documentation is that it is linear, giving the reader little ability to move efficiently around the text, tracking down details.

Unfortunately, software development staff have to carry out a large amount of browsing of project documents. For example, assume that a software system is being maintained by a small project team, and a request comes in to alter the system, say, to increase its functionality. The staff involved in implementing this change have to look at the system specification to ascertain whether the new functions have any affect on any existing functions. They then have to look at those parts of the software design that need to be changed in order to cater for the modification; after that, they have to discover the program code corresponding to the affected design and then modify that. The staff then have to read the system and acceptance test documents to discover what tests need to be rerun, in order to check that the changes made have not created errors that affect the system. Finally, the new system has to be documented and existing documents have to be modified to reflect the change.

Unfortunately, most system documentation is inflexible and very difficult to browse. There is often very poor cross-referencing within documents and little cross-referencing between documents. Because of this, software documentation is often skimped and, eventually, the description of a system, embodied in its documentation, gradually gets out of step with the system itself. This problem is at its most serious during maintenance; however, it often occurs during development on long projects. The result of this, certainly during maintenance, is much more effort required for change than is necessary, and the creation of unnecessary errors.

Advances in software documentation have occurred very slowly. Many software developers were almost funereal in storing project documents on a computer, and taking advantage of the ease of modification that this gives, compared with the standard cut-and-paste techniques used for the last forty years. Now, a major development in database technology threatens to revolutionize the storage and presentation of project documents. The advance is known as hypermedia; it has been made possible by some recent advances in computer hardware.

The essence of a hypermedia document is its ability to support links between parts of the document to other parts, and even to other hypermedia documents. As an example, consider Figure 16.1. It shows part of a hypermedia document used in a stock control application. *Stock details* shows details of parts stocked by a wholesaler. Each part is identified by its name, the number in stock, the supplier and the number that the wholesaler has sold. In *stock details* there are links stored between the name of the supplier and another set of documents that contain details of the supplier: the company name, address, telephone number, and the person to contact when placing an order.

When using this document the stock details might be displayed on a vdu. The user who might wish to find out details of the company that supplied a part would then select the supplier name in the stock details, perhaps by moving a cursor or by dragging an icon over the screen. When the area that contains the link is selected the details it is linked to are then displayed.

This is a very simple example of a hypermedia application. Most hypermedia systems enable a large number of arbitrary links to be set up and maintained.One of the most surprising thing about hypermedia is that its roots lie in the pre-computer age. The man first credited with pointing out its advantages was Vannevar Bush, President Roosevelt's Science Advisor. In an article published in 1945 he called for a post-war effort to mechanize the scientific literature system.[1] In the article he introduced the idea of an automatic browsing machine called memex. Bush described how memex would be used for randomly searching large text corpuses and would also be used to keep notes on the texts that were being browsed. In describing his proposed system Bush recognized the critical part that a link would play, for example, a link between a term in an encyclopaedia and its picture in a book of illustrations.

Bush's work never reached fruition. Computers were unknown in the 1940s; and even in the 1960s computer hardware was not sophisticated enough to support the storage required for linking together documents and the sophisticated graphic interfaces required to access them. However, during the 1970s, mass storage technology became more and more sophisticated, to the point in the 1980s where you can now purchase hard discs with a storage capacity of 20 megabytes for less than £500. Also, increasingly sophisticated display facilities emerged that enable detailed graphics to be displayed, in particular these graphics were associated with workstations manufactured by American companies such as Sun and Apollo.

Much greater definition was achieved in these systems by means of raster graphics. Such graphics are produced by means of dots called pixels being produced and refreshed by programs built into the operating system of the workstation. This provides a much more detailed type of picture than the standard cathode ray tube output devices that were normally associated with the computers of the 1970s.

**Stock Details**

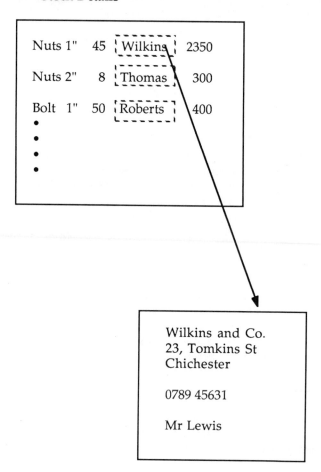

**Figure 16.1**. A simple example of a hypermedia application.

Probably the best known version of hypermedia is the NoteCards system developed at the Xerox Palo Alto Research Centre.[2] The original reason for building this system was to develop an information analyst's workbench that supported the activities of reading sources such as news reports or scholarly articles, collecting information, filing it and writing analytical reports. The architecture of NoteCards is one that programmers can build applications on top of. This enables NoteCards to be customized for a particular application. There are a number of further hypermedia systems [3] including Intermedia developed at Brown University, the Tektronix Neptune, and Boxer. However, the system that threatens to revolutionize the use of hypermedia has recently been released by the computer manufacturers Apple. It is called HyperCard.

There are a number of reasons why HyperCard will revolutionize database technology and threatens to have a massive impact on software projects. The first reason is that it is one of the first hypermedia systems available for a popular computer: the Macintosh. The second reason is that it is cheap. It now comes as a bundled piece of software with all Macintosh computers, and those owners of the Macintosh who bought their computers before HyperCard was released can purchase it in the UK for less than £40.

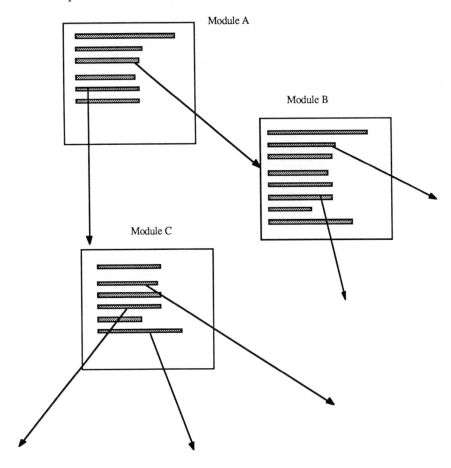

**Figure 16.2.** Part of a HyperCard application.

The heart of any HyperCard application is the stack. A stack consists of a series of cards. Each card contains linking information that allows the user to move from one card to another, or from a card in one stack to a card in another stack. Using the Macintosh this would involve using the mouse device from the computer to select and click buttons on a card that represent the links.

A typical software application for Hypercard is in system design documentation. It is relatively easy to develop a HyperCard application that keeps track of designs. Figure 16.2 shows part of such an application. Each card contains the detailed design of a module. Inside each card there will be links to other modules. Each link shows that the module uses another module that it is linked to. For example, in the figure Module *A* uses Module *B* and Module *C*. Both Module *B* and Module *C* again use other modules in the system. The user of such a document can then navigate around it modifying program text or discovering the vital dependencies that need to discovered during software maintenance.

This model of cards and linkages is quite general; it can be used for any number of applications within a software project and non-software engineering applications. Inside software projects it could be used for all types of documentation; for example, instead of a system design the HyperCard database might consist of each of the functions of a system decomposed into sub-functions, with subfunctions decomposed into sub-subfunctions, and so on.

Outside the software project there are large numbers of applications for hypermedia. Conventional books in which there is a lot of cross-referencing are a natural candidate. Most researchers can relate the frustrations that occur while keeping track of footnotes and references inside heavy tomes.

Teaching texts are also good candidates. A student accessing such a text might want to access a concept that he feels hazy about before proceeding with part of the text, or might want to reread parts of a text before answering a self-assessment question, or might want to gather together particular instances of a concept.

Another area where hypermedia will have a major impact is in conventional data processing. Many applications such as management information systems and personal databases for tasks such as expenses tracking used to require quite sophisticated programs that, previously, could only be provided by technical staff. One of the features of HyperCard is the fact that many applications such as appointments diaries, address books, invoicing programs, and receipting programs can be developed by non-technical staff in a fairly short time.

More sophisticated hypermedia applications usually require some programming. HyperCard is currently released with a programming language called HyperTalk. This is an object-oriented language: typical objects that are manipulated by HyperTalk are cards, buttons that store links, and stacks. Each object is associated with a series of actions that take place when some event occurs during the manipulation of a HyperCard application. For example, assume that a HyperCard application for an address book application has been written, and that an address card contains a series of buttons. The first button moves to the next address card in the stack; the second button, when selected, moves to the previous address card; and the third button might move to a card that contains confidential data on the person whose address is contained in the card containing the button

HyperTalk enables the programmer to designate a button and program its action when, say, it is selected by the mouse attached to the Macintosh. For example, it would be easy to program a button to produce a visual effect such as a slow dissolve, followed by the display, followed by some action such as sending a message to a modem ,which then telephones the person whose card is being accessed.

Object-oriented programming is a very natural style for producing hypermedia applications: so much so, that the massive promise of hypermedia as a non-technical person's database management system could result in an explosion in interest in these languages. There is currently a hiatus in programming language design. Many computer scientists regard conventional programming languages such as Ada and Pascal as the end of an evolutionary chain. However, future fifth-generation languages and logic programming languages are still inefficient on conventional computers, and hardware researchers have yet to produce suitable architectures for these languages. It only requires an explosion of interest in hypermedia to push object-oriented techniques into the fore of language use.

Although hypermedia offers major benefits, there are a number of drawbacks. First, it can be very easy to get lost in a hypermedia document. After following a number of links through a document the user may have little idea where he came from. There used to be a computer game called dungeons and dragons where the player navigated through a labyrinthine maze in order to find a treasure. Many users of hypermedia claim that navigating through a hypermedia document is the same. A number of research groups are attempting to overcome this problem by producing mapping facilities. However, little progress seems yet to have been made and the maps that I have seen have been crude and cumbersome.

The second problem concerns the database structures used for the storage of data in hypermedia application. Currently they are very simple. For example, the stack in a HyperCard application consists of a series of cards held in order, just like a card index. Sophisticated applications require much more complex database systems. One major research area in the next decade should be the grafting of hypermedia front-ends onto conventional database systems, those systems that currently support large-scale applications such as stock control and banking.

My feeling is that hypermedia is still in its early days; and that the first major applications of the technology will be in software documentation. There are a number of reasons for this. First, software projects are usually the first parts of an organization who use sophisticated hardware required to support hypermedia. Second, the amount of browsing and cross-referencing that is required from staff on a software project is considerably more than required in other applications. The amount of time that staff spend in consulting print-outs, designs, and system specifications is orders of magnitude higher than the labour of the the most assiduous seekers after information.

## References

1.    As We May Think, V. Bush, *Atlantic Monthly*, July 1945.

2.    A good description of this system is contained in a paper: NoteCards in a Nutshell, F. G. Halasz, T. P. Moran and T. H. Trigg, *Proceedings of the ACM Conference on Human Factors in Computer Systems.* 1987.

3.    An excellent review of hypermedia technology has been written by Jeff Conklin: Hypertext: An Introduction and Survey, J. Conklin, *Computer*, Sept .1987.

# 17

# Where are we now?

The vast majority of the advances described in the previous pages are still in the research or development stage. Very few of them have impinged on the software industry yet. Where they have, it is usually as the result of a company receiving a grant from a research body or government department to try a particular technique or tool. If the developments do start affecting the way we produce software, as some are bound to, then, based on our experience over the last two decades, the effect on productivity will only be small. As software engineers we always bemoan the fact that we only seem to increase our productivity by a few per cent each year, while our colleagues in the hardware industry seem to increase theirs by an order of magnitude every two or three years.

The reasons for this were described in the first chapter. Software, compared with any other engineered product, is extremely complex, invisible, and easy to change, and has many demands for change placed on it, while the most complex electronic circuit is relatively simple.

In one of the keynote documents about software written in the 1980s,[1] Fred Brookes, a major figure in the development of large-scale software systems, differentiates between two types of difficulty in developing software. The first difficulty is that which arises from the underlying complexity of a software system. The second, less serious difficulty, arises from our propensity to make accidental surface errors in the development of a software system.

Brookes' thesis is that all the developments in the past, and many of those predicted for the future, attack the the second difficulty. Probably the best example of this is the high-level language. In the 1950s the majority of programmers had to struggle with rudimentary programming languages. Often, these languages required the user to write down, and manipulate, patterns of ones and zeros occupying many pages of computer printout. The level of minute detail that the programmer had to concern himself with meant that errors were very easy to make, and the development of anything but the most trivial programs consumed very large amounts of resource. High-level programming languages were developed in the late 1950s in order to overcome this problem. Programming languages, such as COBOL and FORTRAN, replaced patterns of zeros and ones by text that was a lot more understandable and read more like conventional mathematics. In the case of COBOL the programs were even aimed to look like natural language, and to be read by staff such as accountants and finance directors.

The development of high-level languages was a revolutionary step for the software industry. Estimates of its effect on productivity vary; a conservative estimate would be that it increased productivity threefold over twenty years. However, high-level languages only attack the second difficulty: that of our propensity to make surface errors in software development; they do not attack the basic problem of complexity. We now use programming languages of staggering sophistication; however, the problems of late delivery and error-prone software seem much worse than they were twenty years ago. What seems to happen is that as we solve a large number of surface problems, our horizon, in terms of software system size, widens. Consequently, we attempt to develop larger and larger systems, and come up against the major problem of complexity.

In his paper Brookes examines many of the research areas in software engineering that are claimed will greatly increase productivity. For the vast majority he demonstrates that they only solve the surface problems; the only developments that are put forward in his paper as holding out any promise are prototyping, incremental development, and the promotion of good designers.

In Chapter 7 I described how prototyping is able to solve many of the problems associated with eliciting what exactly a customer requires from a computer system; so it it not worth rehearsing a description of the technique here. Incremental development is not new, computer scientists have been urging it on the computer industry since the early 1970s with little success in getting it adopted.[2] It is a management technique for producing large software systems that involves the delivery of successive versions of a system, eventually ending up with the final delivered product.

For example, say a customer wanted a system to carry out stock control for a retail store chain. Such a system would contain facilities for entering details of stock delivered, querying the level of stocks that are available, processing any requests for items to be delivered to a shop, and producing financial statements for the company's management accountants. The first stage in developing such a system incrementally would be to produce a first version that only contains some of the functions that are required. A good set of facilities to implement first would be those concerned with entering the details of stock delivered, since subsequent versions of the software, when tested, will require a database of stock items. The next version of the software system would implement some further functions; for example, it might implement the facilities associated with querying the level of stocks available. The next version of the system would implement further facilities, and so on; finally the whole system would be delivered.

Incremental development has a number of major advantages. First, it enables a version of a system to be developed early on and act as a partial prototype, thus, gaining many of the advantages associated with prototyping. Second, it splits a software project into a series of mini-projects that have the aim of delivering a small tractable piece of software. Not only does this reduce the complexity of the software to be delivered, but it reduces the communicational complexity of the project team. Large project teams spend an inordinate amount of time communicating with each other and, consequently, you find that as more and more staff are added to a project the amount of useful work per capita decreases. The point is often reached where adding an extra member of staff actually decreases the productivity of a project; the effect is analogous to the one described in Chapter 10, where adding a processor to a computer has a much smaller effect on its power than would normally be thought. By using incremental development a large software project can be split into a series of mini-projects, with a relatively small number of staff who do not waste much of their time communicating.

Brookes' final solution to some of the essential problems of software development is to nurture good designers. The designer is one of the key staff in a software project. Even if a project was directed by the most brilliant managers, and was staffed by the best technical programmers, it would pass or fail on the basis of the quality of the design. A design that contains complex interfaces, tortuous logic, and a poor organization of data will easily overcome the talents of managers and development staff, and will give rise to a baroque monster that will suck in more and more resources during maintenance.

The idea that we should nurture good staff by means of careful career development plans, apprenticeships, periods of advanced formal education, and by providing opportunities for them to interact with each other is not that radical. What is radical is its application to technical staff, and software designers in particular. Brookes points out that it is a tradition in industrialized countries to cultivate good managers, but that we do not apply the same principles to technical staff. Certainly, my experience of the career development of technical staff in British industry is that the most many companies will provide for their staff, in career development terms, is the occasional three-day seminar in London, which tends to be regarded, by management and participants alike as more of an opportunity for a shopping spree and a visit to a theatre than as an educational experience.

Brookes' paper will probably become a landmark in 1980s software development, as his management book became in the 1970s. While there is still little proof that the solutions he puts forward (prototyping, incremental development and the nurturing of good designers) will attack the essential problems of software development, his thesis that few past and future techniques will attack the problem seems totally persuasive.

Another reason why we cannot expect to see dramatic increases in productivity in software development is the in-built conservatism inherent in software development. By this I do not mean that staff involved in software development are naturally resistant to the spread of ideas; indeed, I often find the reverse is true. What I mean is that the very nature of software development imposes a conservatism on the high-level management of an information technology company. Almost invariably, such a company has a massive investment in existing software. Millions of pounds will be tied up in the documentation and program code of large systems. Because of the nature of the world that they reflect, these systems will undergo continual change, rather than new systems being produced. Consequently, new notations, such as those associated with mathematics, will take a long time to percolate through to systems development staff.

In Chapter 3 I described how, periodically, a software developer should take a hard look at his software portfolio and, to prevent serious degradation of structure, should redesign and reprogram those parts that are showing their age. This is an ideal opportunity to introduce new notations and new techniques into software development. Unfortunately, few companies do this: orders for new software are still booming and many companies have backlogs of applications that need to be computerized. Consequently, the expertise and notations used for maintaining existing software, which tend to reflect yesterday's technology, act as a restraining force on all but the newest companies.

In Chapter 1 I discussed why developing software has been difficult. Fred Brookes' thesis is that it will always remain so, and furthermore, there may be one or two tentative solutions to the problem of the essential complexity of software systems. This should not bother software engineers. Software development is a new discipline and, viewed from my academic viewpoint, seems to be making greater strides than other engineering disciplines such as automotive engineering, where the basic design of the car has remained the same for decades, and where improvements in areas such as fuel injection and engine technology occur in increments much smaller than those that have occurred in software technology.

However, what is saddening, and potentially dangerous, is the expectation that advances in software development should occur at a breakneck speed. A common story told by software developers is of the manager who, when confronted by a software project plan, is mystified why a software system of ten thousand lines of program code takes much longer than a hundred times the length of time taken by his son to write a hundred-line program for his home computer.

Why do we expect software development to be easy and advances to enable orders of magnitude improvements in efficiency? One factor is, of course, education. It saddens me that colleagues of mine, who are convincing in the seminar environment, are unable, or unwilling, to communicate the problems of software development to a larger audience via the medium of print. Another factor is that software is closely associated with hardware, and certainly the latter has made gigantic strides over the last two decades. The computer that I am typing this text into is orders of magnitude more powerful than the computer I learned programming on twenty years ago: it processes programs faster, has two orders of magnitude more main memory and has, for my purposes, an unlimited off-line storage capacity.

Unfortunately, many people forget that computer circuits, compared with even medium-size software systems, are extremely simple. One of the standard presentation slides that I often see from academics who are attempting to demonstrate the effectiveness of a particular method, notation, or tool, shows two curves: one indicating advances in hardware technology, the other showing advances in software technology. The former is exponential, and soon disappears off the slide; the latter seems almost to be a straight line that would disappear only if the slide were a few miles in length.

It is much more realistic to hail our hardware colleagues' staggering achievements. They are still at the stage that the early automotive engineers were at eighty years ago, when large advances could be made in car design, advances that pushed speeds from a walking pace to over thirty miles per hour. To use their achievements as a stick to beat software developers only creates a false impression of the possible advances that could be made for the remainder of this century.

A further reason for the widespread impression that software developers should be making great strides is that the computer industry is still the victim of large amounts of hyperbole. It is a young industry where novel products emerge weekly, and where it is still possible for small software companies to challenge much larger companies and each other. Consequently, the market place is a much noisier place than normal. Unfortunately, the backlog of applications is so large that many customers for software tools and methods seem to want fast solutions. In such circumstances, the people to consult about whether the volume knob is turned up too high in the market place are academics.

Unfortunately, the habit of overestimating the gains from new techniques, methods and tools seems to have spread to the academic world. I attend a large number of conferences, and one of the marked phenomena that I have observed over the last five years in software researchers is an absence of doubt. It is too easy to parody the academic's legitimate concern with the truth as he sees it, by the academic who, in reaching a simple, one-sentence conclusion, prefaces that conclusion with many thousands of words of convoluted exceptions, dependencies and pre-conditions. Nevertheless, it is the role of the academic to take a dispassionate, even sceptical, approach to evaluating developments in his field. This we seem to be falling down on.

The reason, certainly in the United Kingdom, is that, for the universities, the economic climate is very harsh. Academics tend to be judged on their ability to attract grant funding, rather than their ability to carry out thoughtful research or book writing. It has lead to the phenomenon of the professor-impresario travelling the world and being involved in time-consuming and tiring meetings to garner funds for the next research project.

I am not implying that finding funds is an intrinsically evil process. An academic who wishes to carry out research in computer science needs money for computer equipment, and for staff such as research assistants. What I am saying is that since an increasing amount of that funding is coming from industry, and from governments with a perspective that stretches no further than the next election, then it is a very brave academic who, in seeking funds, or declaiming that his way is the best, would temper his messages with warnings and pre-conditions, and without worrying about the wider context outside the software project. Consequently, a number of advances in software engineering have, over the past decade, been put forward as saviours of the software developer and have yet to fully realize their promise.

Two examples illustrate this. The first is the use of formal methods in software development. The use of mathematics to specify the function of a software system is intuitively appealing. Many of the ills in the software project can be attributed to poor statements of requirements and system specifications. Mathematics has the property of exactness that is required for software documentation. Yet, little progress has been made in the last four years, even though documents emanating from the Department of Trade's Alvey Programme in its early days were predicting that within the time span of the project (five years), 30% of the applications written in this country would use mathematics. Today that target looks extremely unlikely. Those few projects that use mathematics in our country are, almost invariably, supported by grants from governmental bodies. Only a handful of software developers — I would guess less than 1% — are willing to bet real money on innovation.

In observing this phenomenon, it is all too easy to blame anti-intellectualism on the part of industry, or to point out their poor record of innovation. However, the reasons are usually much deeper. Obviously, some of the brakes on innovation described above are to blame for this: in particular the conservatism forced on software developers by massive investment in current software notations is one major factor. However, there are serious extra-technological reasons why mathematics has not progressed. First, there is the fact that by basing software development on mathematics a real engineering profession would emerge. Many staff who call themselves software engineers forget that one of the major characteristics of an engineering process is the use of science and mathematics as a base for building artefacts within cost limits. Such an engineering discipline would threaten the career structure of virtually every software development company in the United Kingdom.

The second reason is that the mathematics that underpins formal methods of software development is quite new to the vast majority of practitioners. Many of them have studied mathematics, but only the type of mathematics that can help in disciplines such as automotive engineering or civil engineering. Finite mathematics — the mathematics of discrete steps, suited to describing computers that process ones or zeros — is still virtually an unknown subject to many staff in the software industry. There is thus a training problem that is quite large.

Many of the proponents of mathematics on software projects that I meet admit to me that training is a problem. However, the solution, a fortnight course at a local university followed by a number of months of work on a project using mathematics, still seriously underestimates the problem. To write elegant mathematical descriptions of software systems requires a large amount of teaching, and the process of proving, mathematically, that a system has desired properties, requires a degree of sophistication that only comes after a year or two of practice.

Thus, the comparative failure of mathematics to progress on software projects seems not to be caused by any technological deficiencies, but by ignoring and not addressing some major economic, social, and educational questions.

A second example of overselling is taken from the expert system arena. In general the expert systems which have been successful have been developed for very limited domains, where the underlying factors can be easily quantified. For example, successful expert systems have been written to diagnose diseases on the basis of factors such as patient temperature, respiratory rate, blood-sample analyses, and blood pressure; all quantities easily expressed in numerical terms. However, expert system technology has been proposed for relatively fuzzy areas such as psychiatry, sociometrics and the law.

One recent controversy over the use of experts systems and the law illustrates the problems of overestimating the utility of a particular technique. In the mid 1980s a team at Imperial College London, lead by Professor Robert Kowalski, the father of logic programming, carried out research into the computerization of the English Nationality Act. The aim of the research was to develop an expert system that advised potential immigrants as to their status as legal visitors to the United Kingdom.

What the team did was to study the nationality act and store it as the type of production system that is described in Chapter 6. Their system was hailed as an impressive advance in expert system technology, until in 1986 a young researcher in the Department of Jurisprudence at Queens University, Belfast, Phillip Leith, produced a damning paper that was a powerful indictment of that research. The paper was published in the ultra-respectable journal of the British Computer Society and caused a storm in the expert system community. Leith's message was direct, in the abstract to the paper he stated that:

> ... the team have a muddled view of the legal process and the usefulness of logic programming in that field, and suggest that this incorrect perspective might well pervade into other areas in which the team claim success.[3]

The essence of the paper, in which legal case law was continually invoked in support, was that the idea of viewing the law as a set of clear rules, as the Imperial College team did, was to take a grossly simplistic view of the legal process. In demolishing the Imperial College work, Leith pointed out that there was a long history of judges ignoring rules in making decisions, that the British Nationality Act was also subject to other legal processes, in particular those emanating from the European Courts of Justice, and that there were whole parts of the law that were not part of the legislation.

When the facts about the Imperial College work emerged it turned out that in attempting to computerize the legal process they had not fully involved any experts in the mechanics of the legal system. While attempts to carry technological advances into fuzzy areas such as the law are valuable in defining the limits of technology, it is not difficult to see that a better approach would have been to have involved lawyers and experts in legal philosophy, rather than set out on a potentially expensive development of a large software system. What I suspect happened is that the Imperial College team affected, by the considerable glamour that was attached to expert systems because of Japanese interest, assumed that the technology was so powerful that it could overcome any difficulties outside a purely technological framework.

The danger here is that of a promising technology being abandoned because of its inability to live up to grossly unrealistic expectations. Expert systems are certainly a good example of this. They were promoted widely in the early 1980s and hailed as an extremely powerful technology. Now, in 1988, we see that their spread into industry has been very slow. The temptation is, of course, to regard the area as a technological cul-de-sac. However, as I have tried to indicate in Chapter 15, there are many useful, but mundane, applications of expert systems that are completely different from their use as a repository of knowledge and an electronic brain. The danger is that any reaction against failures in their use as an electronic brain will result in resistance to their use as mundane software systems.

This, then, is software development in the 1980s: considerable expectations from the public and from industry, a large amount of hyperbole generated by companies attempting to sell their products on the open market, and also by academics, with reality being a few percent gain in productivity each year. No magic tools, techniques, or methods have yet to emerge, and, given the nature of software, such a breakthrough would be an intellectual step forward equivalent to the invention of the motor engine.

However, what must not be forgotten is the result of the gradual increases in productivity since the 1950s. We now develop large software systems that control the businesses of transcontinental corporations, that predict the weather, fly combat planes without pilot intervention, manage movements of hundreds of airliners, and simulate nuclear reactors. There are very few examples of serious errors in such systems, the main stress of current research being to improve productivity. It is a testament to the flexibility and resilience of the human mind that the baroque software constructions that emerge from industry are on the whole safe and reliable.

# References

1.  No Silver Bullet — Essence and Accidents of Software Engineering, F. P. Brookes Jr., *IEEE Computer*, 4. 1987.
2.  Top-down Programming in Large Systems, in *Debugging Techniques in Large Systems,* R. Ruston (Ed.), Englewood Cliffs, N.J.: Prentice Hall. 1971
3.  Fundamental Errors in Logic Programming, P. Leith, *Computer Journal*, **29**, 6. 1986.

# Index